HORRIBLE HISTORIES

TERRIBLE TUDORS

TERRY DEARY & NEIL TONGE

ILLUSTRATED BY **MARTIN BROWN**

■ **SCHOLASTIC**

For Stephen

Scholastic Children's Books,
Euston House, 24 Eversholt Street,
London, NW1 1DB, UK

A division of Scholastic Ltd
London ~ New York ~ Toronto ~ Sydney ~ Auckland
Mexico City ~ New Delhi ~ Hong Kong

First published in the UK by Scholastic Ltd, 1993
This edition published in the UK by Scholastic Ltd, 2008

ISBN 978 1407 10738 7

Printed by Leo Paper Products, China

2 4 6 8 10 9 7 5 3 1

CONTENTS

Introduction 7

The terrible Tudors 9

Terrible Tudor times 16

Terrible Tudor life and death 20

Terrible Tudor schools 26

Tudor crimes ... and terrible punishments 35

Terrible Shakespeare 52

Terrible Tudor mystery 58

Terrible Tudor kings and queens 64

Terrible Tudor witches 80

Terrible Tudor food 89

Terrible Tudor fun and games 95

Terrible Tudor sailors 104

Terrible Tudor clothes 114

Terrible Tudor life for women 119

Epilogue 125

Grisly Quiz 127

Interesting Index 135

Introduction

If you think history is horrible then this is the book for you!

Sometimes history lessons in school can be horribly boring...

Sometimes it can be horribly confusing...

And sometimes history can be **horribly** unfair…

But this book is about **really horrible** history. It's full of the sort of facts that teachers never bother to tell you. Not just the bits about the kings and the queens and the battles and the endless lists of dates - it's also about the ordinary people who lived in Tudor times. People like you and me. Commoners! (Well, I'm dead common, I don't know about you!)

And what made them laugh and cry, what made them suffer and die. **That's what this book will try to help you understand.** You might learn some things your teachers don't even know! (Believe it or not, **teachers do not know everything!**)

There are one or two activities you can try. That's about the best way to find out what it was like to be a common Tudor.

There are some stories that are as chilling as the chilliest horror stories in your library. (You may have to read them with the light turned off in case you are scared of the shadows!) The facts and the stories should amaze you and teach you and amuse you, and sometimes make you sad.

Hopefully you'll find them all **horribly interesting**.

The terrible Tudors

What is a terrible Tudor?

What your teacher will tell you…
The Tudors were a family who ruled England, and poked their noses into the rest of Great Britain, from 1485 till 1603. The grandfather was Henry VII, his son was Henry VIII and the grandchildren were Edward VI, Mary I and Elizabeth I.

Five rulers and 118 years that changed the lives of the English people.

Who's who?

HENRY VII

Henry VII (Henry Tudor of Lancaster) King from 1485 to 1509
Defeated King Richard III at the Battle of Bosworth and took his crown. Married Elizabeth of York to stop their two families whingeing scrapping over the crown.

Henry VIII King from 1509 to 1547
Son of Henry VII. Wanted a son to keep the Tudor line going and he didn't care how many wives he had till he got one.

HENRY VIII

When he got rid of his first wife by divorcing her, the head of the Catholic Church (the Pope I didn't approve of it ... so Henry made his own church (the Church of England), with himself as the head.

Henry got rid of the Catholic monasteries with their monks and nuns. (The money he got for their riches came in very handy!) But he still worshipped as a Catholic, and chopped off the heads of those who didn't.

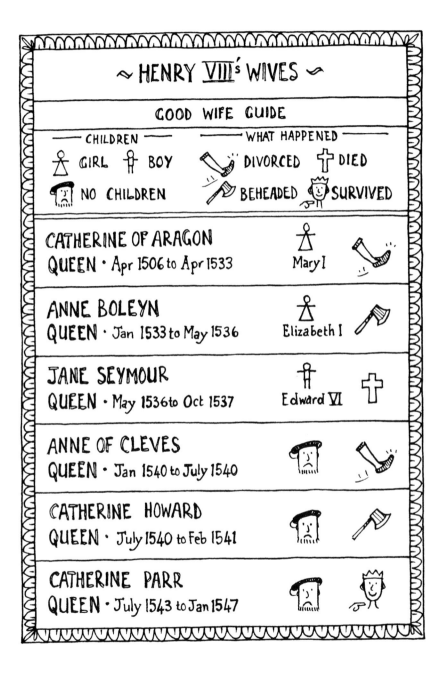

~ HENRY VIII's WIVES ~

GOOD WIFE GUIDE

CHILDREN — GIRL · BOY · NO CHILDREN

WHAT HAPPENED — DIVORCED · DIED · BEHEADED · SURVIVED

CATHERINE OF ARAGON
QUEEN · Apr 1506 to Apr 1533 — Mary I — *divorced*

ANNE BOLEYN
QUEEN · Jan 1533 to May 1536 — Elizabeth I — *beheaded*

JANE SEYMOUR
QUEEN · May 1536 to Oct 1537 — Edward VI — *died*

ANNE OF CLEVES
QUEEN · Jan 1540 to July 1540 — *no children* — *divorced*

CATHERINE HOWARD
QUEEN · July 1540 to Feb 1541 — *no children* — *beheaded*

CATHERINE PARR
QUEEN · July 1543 to Jan 1547 — *no children* — *survived*

Anne Boleyn's last words before she had her head chopped off were **not**, "I'll just go for a walk around the block!"

Edward became king first, even though he was the youngest. That's because a male child always took the throne before a female child. The same rule still applies in England.

EDWARD VI

Edward VI King of England from 1547 to 1553
Was too young to rule, so had a Protector, the Duke of Somerset, to "help" him out. King Edward was engaged to Mary Queen of Scots, but this fell through. Just as well, really, as Edward was a Protestant and Mary a Catholic, which would have caused big problems. The Duke of Northumberland, made Edward get rid of Somerset. Northumberland became the next Protector - what a surprise! Poor Edward was a sickly lad and died of tuberculosis at the age of 16.

Lady Jane Grey Queen of England in 1553
Put on the throne by Northumberland, who had persuaded Edward to make her his heir because she was a Protestant, and was great grand-daughter of Henry VII. She was also Northumberland's daughter-in-law! Lady Jane sat on the throne for nine days then Mary Tudor raised an army and walloped Northumberland. So Lady Jane was pushed off her throne and her head was pushed on the block.

LADY JANE GREY

Mary I (Mary Tudor) Queen of England 1553 to 1558
Was a devout Catholic, so she made the Pope head of the English church again. Married King Philip of Spain, also a Catholic. People were frightened of Philip's power, and the marriage led to Wyatt's rebellion, which was crushed by Mary's army. Philip, never short of an idea or two, persuaded Mary to fight the French. The English lost. Mary was getting more unpopular by the minute, but was probably too insane to care. Ended up with the nickname 'Bloody Mary', owing to regular head-choppings and burnings of Protestants.

MARY I
(MARY TUDOR)

ELIZABETH I

Elizabeth I Queen of England from 1558 to 1603
Had pretended to be a Catholic while Mary Tudor was Queen, just to keep her happy. But changed both herself and England into Protestants when she came to the throne. Locked up Mary Queen of Scots and chopped off her head because she was a Catholic, and because Catholic Europe thought that Mary should be Queen of England. Elizabeth never married, because she said that she was married to England! But she had a definite soft spot for the Earl of Essex, which didn't stop her from having **his** head chopped off as well.

Terrible Tudor Limericks

Confused? You may be, but try learning these limericks, and you'll easily remember…

Henry VII
Henry Tudor beat Richard the Thirder
When the battle turned into pure murder.
Henry pinched Richard's crown
For the ride back to town.
He was top man! He could go no furder.

Henry VIII
King Henry was fat as a boar
He had six wives and still wanted more.
Anne and Kate said,
"By heck! He's a pain in the neck!"
As their heads landed smack on the floor.

Edward VI
At nine years the little King Eddie
Had a grip on the throne quite unsteady.
He was all skin and bone,
Grown men fought for his throne
And by sixteen young Eddie was deadie.

Mary I

Bloody Mary, they say, was quite mad.
And the nastiest taste that she had
Was for protestant burning
Seems she had a yearning
To kill even more than her dad.

Elizabeth I

A truly great queen was old Lizzie,
She went charging around being busy.
She thought herself beaut,
But her teeth looked like soot
And her hair it was all red and frizzy.

Terrible Tudor times

1485 - reign of Henry VII

Henry Tudor beat King Richard III at the Battle of Bosworth Field and became the first Tudor king. The Wars of the Roses ended - they had been dividing the country for over 30 years.
1487 A boy called Lambert Simnel claims to be king. His revolt fails. Is given a job in the palace kitchens!
1492 Christopher Columbus lands in America - the world is never the same again!

1497 Perkin Warbeck tries to take the English throne. Warbeck hanged in 1499. England settles down under Henry VII and becomes richer and more peaceful than in the past.

1509 - reign of Henry VIII

1516 Mary I born - daughter of Henry VIII's Catholic first wife, Catherine of Aragon.
1517 First real Protestant revolt against the Catholic Church begins in Germany.

1520 Henry VIII appears at the Field of the Cloth of Gold - a ceremonious meeting between Henry and Francis I of France.

1533 Elizabeth I born, daughter of Henry's second wife, Anne Boleyn.

1534 Henry takes over as head of the Church in England.

1535 Henry begins to execute Catholics who object to his Church takeover.

1536 Anne Boleyn, (Elizabeth I's mother) executed and Henry begins to close down monasteries. 1537 Edward VI born - but his mother dies shortly afterwards. Edward is always a weak child.

1547 - reign of Edward VI

1547 Edward VI just nine years old when he takes the throne.

The Duke of Somerset runs the country for the boy. His title is 'Protector'.

1549 Kett's rebellion in Norfolk against the new Protestant king.

1550 The Duke of Somerset executed and replaced by Duke of Northumberland as the new Protector.

17

1553 Edward is ill. He is persuaded to name Lady Jane Grey as the next Queen – this is partly to stop the Catholic Mary getting her hands on the throne … but the plan doesn't work. Young Ed dies.

1553 – reign of Mary I

Mary tries to return England to the Catholic faith. She has over 300 Protestants burned.
1556 Thomas Cranmer, Henry VIII and Edward VI's Protestant Archbishop of Canterbury, burned at the stake for opposing Mary.

1558 The English lose Calais (in France) to the French people. Mary unpopular for this and for her marriage to the Catholic Philip II of Spain. Luckily she dies before she is overthrown!

1558 – reign of Elizabeth I

1564 William Shakespeare born.
1567 Mary Queen of Scots thrown off her throne. She flees to England a year later.
1568 England and Spain begin to argue over control of the oceans.

1577 Francis Drake begins his voyage round the world - returns in 1580.
1587 Mary Queen of Scots executed.
1588 The Spanish Armada tries to invade England but is defeated.
1601 The Earl of Essex rebels against Elizabeth and is executed.

1603

End of Terrible Tudors - in come the Slimy Stuarts.

Kett's Rebellion

In Norfolk, 1549, the problem was too many sheep and too few jobs. The grumbles grew into a revolt. The revolting Norfolk men were led by the most revolting Robert Kett - a local landowner. But Robert's rebels grew hungry and weak. Edward VI sent the Earl of Warwick to deal with them. The Earl cut the rebels to pieces ... but they weren't as cut up as Robert Kett might have been. He was sentenced to...

... be dragged to Tyburn, where he is to be hung and whilst still alive his entrails taken out and burned before him, his head cut off and his body cut into four pieces.

As it happened, Robert was taken to Norfolk Castle and hung in chains over the battlements.

Terrible Tudor life and death

Life begins at 40

Would **you** like to have lived in Tudor times? A 1980 school history book said … *All in all the Elizabethan Age was an extremely exciting time to be alive.* But this is a *Horrible History* book. You make up your own mind about how "exciting" it was when you have the real facts. For example … You probably know a lot of people who are 40 years old, or older. But would you have known as many in Tudor times?

Imagine that ten children were born on a particular day in a Tudor town. How many do you think would still be alive to celebrate their 40th birthdays?

a) 6   b) 9   c) 1   d) 4

Answer: c. On average, only one person in ten lived to the age of 40. Many died in childhood – the first year was the most dangerous of your life.

Why were Tudor times so unhealthy? Perhaps these will help you understand…

Half a dozen filthy facts

1 Open sewers ran through the streets and carried diseases.
2 Toilets were little more than a hole in the ground outside the back door.

3 Water came from village pumps. These often took the water from a local river, and that river was full of the filth from the town.

4 Country people made their own medicines from herbs, or went to an "apothecary". People still use herbal cures today … but would you take one from a Tudor apothecary who didn't know the importance of washing their hands before handling your medicine?

5 A popular cure for illness was "blood-letting". Most people believed that too much blood made you ill. All you had to do was lose some and you'd feel better. Where could you go to lose some blood? The local barber. (He had a part-time job as a surgeon when he wasn't cutting hair!) Sometimes the barber would make a deep cut; other times a scratch was made, followed by a heated cup over the wound to "suck" the blood out.

6 Some doctors used slimy, blood-sucking creatures called leeches to suck blood out of the patient. (And some doctors today still use leeches to cure certain blood diseases!)

Doctor, doctor…!

If you were a doctor in Tudor times, what cures would you suggest for illnesses?

Here are ten illnesses - and ten Tudor cures. Match the cure to the illness…

1. HEADACHE

A. Shave the head and smear with the grease of a fox. Or, wash the head with the juice of beetles. Or, crush garlic rub it in the head and wash in vinegar

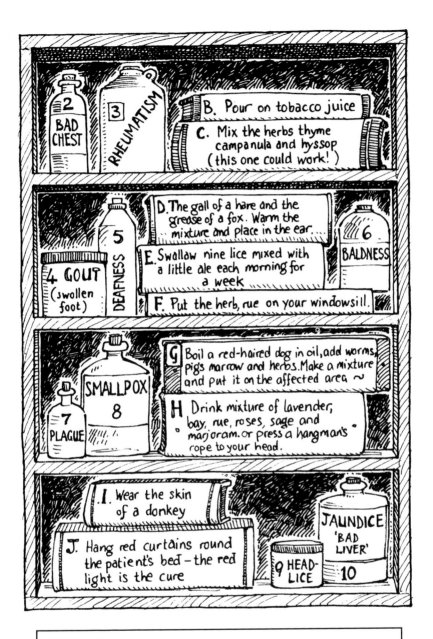

2 BAD CHEST

3 RHEUMATISM

B. Pour on tobacco juice

C. Mix the herbs thyme campanula and hyssop (this one could work!)

4 GOUT (swollen foot)

5 DEAFNESS

6 BALDNESS

D. The gall of a hare and the grease of a fox. Warm the mixture and place in the ear....

E. Swallow nine lice mixed with a little ale each morning for a week

F. Put the herb, rue on your windowsill.

7 PLAGUE

SMALLPOX 8

G. Boil a red-haired dog in oil, add worms, pig's marrow and herbs. Make a mixture and put it on the affected area ~

H. Drink mixture of lavender, bay, rue, roses, sage and marjoram. or press a hangman's rope to your head.

I. Wear the skin of a donkey

J. Hang red curtains round the patient's bed – the red light is the cure

9 HEAD-LICE

JAUNDICE 'BAD LIVER' 10

Answers: 1=H 2=C 3=I 4=G 5=D 6=A 7=F 8=J 9=B 10=E

23

How did you do, Doctor? It wouldn't really matter if you got them all wrong. Most of them wouldn't have worked anyway!

Patient, patient...!

If you were sick in those extremely exciting Tudor times, which would you rather do?
Feel sick ... or try one of these extremely exciting Tudor cures?

Ten cures you wouldn't want to try...

1 Swallow powdered human skull.

2 Eat live spiders (covered in butter to help them slide down a little easier). Swallowing young frogs was suggested as a cure for asthma.

3 Fustigation - the patient is given a good beating,

4 Throw a stone over your house - but the stone must first

have killed a man, a wild boar or a she-bear.

5 Eat the scrapings from the skull of an executed criminal.

6 Eat bone-marrow mixed with sweat.

7 Sniff sneezing-powder to clear the head.

8 Have burning hot plasters placed on the body to raise blisters.

9 Mix the blood from a black cat's tail with cream, then drink it.

10 Place half a newly-killed pigeon on plague sores.

Nowadays we know that the dreadful plagues were carried by fleas. The Tudors didn't know about the disease they carried. Still, they weren't keen on fleas because they bit and made you itch. They had a cure you might like to try if you ever have them in your bedroom...

First, to gather all the fleas of thy chamber into one place, cover a staff with the grease of a fox or a hedgehog. Lay the staff in thy chamber and it shall gather all the fleas to it. Also, fill a dish with goat's blood and put it by the bed and all the fleas will come to it.

DON'T SLURP!

Fleas love to bite humans to get at their blood. They might well dash off to a whole dish of goat's blood!

Terrible Tudor schools

Parents, grandparents, teachers and other old fogeys... they all do it. They all talk about "The Good Old Days". Then they go on to talk about how terrible it was in school. They say things like... When I was a young lad/lass/goldfish just knee high to a grasshopper/grass hut/grass skirt schools were schools. You kids have it easy these days. We used to get a caning/whipping/sweet if we as much as opened our mouth/eyes/door. We had 6/12/25 hours of homework every night and we were kept in detention/ prison/vinegar until we did it. They. were the best days of our lives!"

If they think **their** schools were tough it's as well they didn't go to school in Tudor times. (Or maybe they did and they're lying when they tell you they're only 39.) If they had they would know that...

1 Most village children didn't go to school. A few might attend a "Dame" school run by a local dame (woman).

2 Children rarely had books. They may have had "Horn" books, though. These were pieces of wood the shape and size of a table-tennis bat. On one side was a printed page with the alphabet and perhaps, the Lord's Prayer. The other side was blank and could be used to practise writing.

'HORN' BOOK FOR SHORTSIGHTED PUPILS

3 Richer children could be sent away to school. At first, the monks in the monasteries ran most of the schools, known as choir schools. Henry VIII closed the monasteries because they were run by the Catholic Church. He started a new church, the Church of England, but he lost the schools in

the process, and was left with only a handful of grammar schools. He had to encourage new ones to be set up, but in fact only 20 more grammar schools were established during his reign. So much for education!

How does your school compare with a Tudor school? Check out these Tudor school rules and decide...

What to expect at school

Timetable

School lessons went on from dawn till sunset with a break for school dinners.

(If you lived a long way from school, you'd have to get up in the dark to allow time for walking. The roads were muddy, cold and dangerous on the short winter days.)

~ SCHOOL RULES ~

No scholar shall wear a dagger or any other weapon. They shall not bring to school any stick or bat, only their meat knife.

Manchester Grammar School 1528
It is ordered that for every oath or rude word spoken, in the school or elsewhere, the scholar shall have three strokes of the cane.

Oundle School 1566
Scholars shall not go to taverns or ale-houses and must not play unlawful games such as cards, dice or the like.

Hawkshead School 1585
Punishment for losing your school cap . . . a beating
Punishment for making fun of another pupil . . . a beating.

THAT'S A MEAT KNIFE?

#6!!✓

HA HA HA

School swots

Working hard at school was not always popular with the upper-class parent.

One father said, *I'd rather see my son hanged than be a bookworm. It is a gentleman's life to hunt and to hawk. A gentleman should leave learning to clodhoppers.*

~ SCHOOL MEALS ~

Breakfast
Bread and butter and a little fruit

Lunch
Rye bread, salted meat and ale

Tea
Bread with dried fruit and nuts – fresh fruit in summer

Rules at meal times
1 Wear a cap to keep your hair out of your food.
2 Don't wipe your mouth with your hand or sleeve.
3 Don't let your sleeve drag in your food.
4 Don't lean on the table.
5 Don't pick your teeth with your pen-knife or your fork.
Punishment for breaking a rule . . . a beating.

WHERE'S MY CAP?

School teachers

Their job (in Westminster School at least) was to see that their pupils:

behave themselves properly in church and school as well as in games, that their faces and hands are washed, their heads combed, their hair and nails cut, their clothes and shoes kept clean so that no lice or dirt may infect themselves or their companions.

School punishments

Schoolmasters would often beat their pupils. Henry Peachum wrote,

I know one who in winter would, on a cold morning, whip his boys for no other reason than to warm himself up. Another beat them for swearing, and all the while he swore himself with horrible oaths.

But they weren't all so bad. The headmaster of Eton in 1531 was Nicholas Udall. He wrote the first English play that wasn't religious, and it was also the first comedy play.

School holidays

No long holidays. Schools would close for 16 days at Christmas and 12 days at Easter, but there were no summer holidays.

Lessons

A class might have as many as 60 pupils. Many hours were spent learning long passages from textbooks by heart. This not only kept them all quiet - it also saved having to buy books! Main subjects: Latin, Arithmetic, Divinity (Religious Study), English Literature.

School sports

A Shrove Tuesday custom was to take money to school, and with it the schoolmaster would buy a fighting cock. The master put a long string on the cock and tied it to a post. Boys would then take turns at throwing a stick at the cock. If a boy hit then the cock became his - if every boy hit then the cock belonged to the schoolmaster.

School equipment

Pupils had to write with quill pens made from feathers. These would have to be sharpened with a knife nearly every day. The small knife used was called a pen-knife - and we can still buy "penknives" today … even if we don't sharpen our ballpoints with them.

If you'd really like to know what it was like to write with a quill pen then you could try making one.

You need

1. A strong feather - goose quill is best, but turkey or any other strong feather will do.

2. A pen-knife - if you haven't a pen-knife then a Stanley knife will be just as good.

3. Tweezers.

4. Ink.

And an adult to make sure you don't get chopped fingers on the table!

How to make it

1. Shorten the feather to about 20cm.

2. Strip off all the barbs (the feathery part) from the shaft.

(Yes, I know! In all the pictures you've seen the writers appear to be writing with feathers. They hardly ever did they only used the shaft and threw the rest away. Honest!)

3 Cut the bottom of the shaft off with your pen-knife (Figure 1).

4 Shape the bottom of the shaft as in Figure 2. Take out the core with tweezers.

5 Make a slit at the end of the nib about 5mm long (Figure 3).

6 Trim the end of the shaft again, this time at an angle. (Figure 4 shows the angle for a right-handed writer)

7 Dip the quill in ink. Try writing an alphabet.

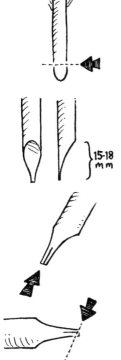

15-18 mm

ABCDE ᴘ Gh 👁Jk l m

Test your teacher on Tudors

Here are a couple of facts your teacher (or parents or friends) may **think** they know. Perhaps you'll catch them out if you ask…

1 The first post

You: Please, Miss! (or Sir, or Fatface) Who had the first postal service in this country?

Teacher: I'm glad you asked me that…

(Teachers are always glad when you ask them something - it makes them think you are interested.)

… Of course, everybody knows that the famous Victorian, Rowland Hill, invented the postal service.

You: (with a sigh) But my book on the Terrible Tudors says the first postal service was invented in the reign of Elizabeth the First!

Then go on to quote these facts…

Rowland Hill created the Penny Post and postage stamps, not the postal service. Tudor Guilds and universities had private postal services. The government was worried about spies sending messages out of the country this way. So they insisted that a service under The Master of Posts should carry all letters sent outside England - that way they could read them if they suspected something!

2 A miss is as good as a mile

You: Please, Sir! (or Miss, or Fairy-features) If you asked Henry VIII how many yards there are in a mile, what would he say?

Teacher: I'm glad you asked me that... He would say 1,760 yards, of course.

You: That's not what my book on the Terrible Tudors says. It says that if you asked Henry VIII how many yards there are in a mile he would say, "It depends where you are."

Teacher: Eh!?!

You: (Explain) It wasn't till Queen Elizabeth's reign that a mile was fixed at 1,760 yards. Before that it depended on where you lived.

LONDON MILE = 5,000 yards
ENGLISH MILE = 6,610 yards
WELSH MILE - about 4 modern miles
IRISH MILE = 2,240 yards
SCOTTISH MILE = 1,976 yards

I THOUGHT YOU MIGHT HAVE KNOWN THAT, MISS!

Then count your lucky stars that you aren't in school in Tudor times!

Tudor crime ... and terrible punishments

In Britain in 1992 crime was the fourth largest "business" in the country - people on both sides of the law made 14 billion pounds. In Tudor times it must have been as bad, with more than 10,000 homeless beggars on the city streets. Many were simply rogues who tricked, cheated and stole from kindhearted people who thought they were helping the poor. Yes, there were more crimes in those days, ... and more punishments. Some of them seem incredible today.

Thieving

Humphrey Lisle's story - Newcastle, 1528

Humphrey Lisle must have been worried. Dead worried.
He knew the English laws of 1528: steal up to eleven pence
and you went to prison. Steal twelve pence (one shilling) or
more ... and you could be hanged. Humphrey had been one
of a gang of Scottish raiders who'd stolen much more than
twelve pence. One of the charges against Humphrey said
that he ...

*at Gosforth, a mile from Newcastle, took prisoner twenty-seven
people passing by in the High Street, from whom he took 26
shillings and 8 pence. He ransomed all but seven whom he kept
for a while as slaves in Scotland.*

Stealing twenty-seven shillings! Kidnapping! Slavery!
Humphrey and the gang had been caught and locked up in
Newcastle jail. The gang were the worst villains in the North
and now they were safely in chains in prison.

They were still in chains when they went to court. One by
one the judge sentenced them to death. Humphrey's father
was sentenced to death first. Then it was Humphrey's turn.
"You admit to all the charges against you?" the judge asked.
"Aye, sir," Humphrey answered.
"But I am not going to sentence you to death," the judge went
on.
A gasp of surprise went around the court. They had been
looking forward to seeing Humphrey's head stuck on a pole
on the town walls. It was just what he deserved, wasn't it?
The Newcastle people couldn't understand why the judge
spared Humphrey's life.

Can you give a reason for the judge sparing Humphrey s life?
Was it because…

1 Humphrey had friends outside who threatened to have the judge killed?

2 Humphrey was very rich and offered the judge a lot of money?

3 Humphrey was the youngest in the gang and the judge wanted to give him a second chance?

4 Humphrey was Scottish and so was the judge?

Answer: 3. Humphrey Lisle was just twelve years old when he joined the gang that stole, burned, murdered and kidnapped its way through the north. The judge took pity on him. Within a few years Humphrey Lisle was working for the English … helping to catch Scottish raiders!

Believing is a crime

Tudor people were very concerned with religion. It was important to the kings and queens, to the people and to the law. Catholicism was the religion of England and most European countries until the 16th century.

But the invention of the printing press in the 15th century meant that more and more people had access to the Bible and were beginning to question the wisdom of priests. Ordinary folk were expected to believe all sorts of things, and were encouraged to buy "relics". These were things like bits of old bone and hair that some priests said belonged to saints. Yuk! Anyway, all this led to people wanting change within the Church.

And some kings and queens, who wanted absolute power without interference from Catholic leaders, were only too happy to encourage this change, which was known as the Reformation. The "reformists" were generally known as Protestants. There was a lot of hatred between the Catholics and the Protestants.

Catholics wanted...

The Pope as head of the church - services in Latin churches decorated with paintings and statues.

Protestants wanted ... No Pope - services in English - plain churches.

Often, the hatred between them was terribly deadly...

Margaret Clitheroe's story - York, 1586

Margaret Clitheroe was a Catholic. In the days of Elizabeth I that was not a safe thing to be. But a lot of Catholics kept their religion and stayed secure by playing safe. They went to the Church of England services as the law said they had to. They kept their Catholic beliefs quietly to themselves.

But Margaret Clitheroe was not that sort of woman. She was a "recusant" - she refused to go to a protestant church.

Her husband, John, was a rich butcher in the city of York. "Margaret," he sighed, "the officers of the law cannot ignore you any longer. They will take you to court and fine you. Come to church with me today. It can't do you any harm!"

But Margaret was stubborn. "No, John." He shook his head and left for church. He walked by Micklegate Bar, one of the main gates of York. The remains of executed Catholics were still hanging there, more grisly than anything on his butcher's stall. He shuddered and wished his wife would learn some sense.

He'd have been still more worried had he known that Margaret was doing more than just missing church. She was also hiding Catholic priests in their house. But not for much longer.

The officers had started questioning people who knew Margaret Clitheroe. They were trying to make a case against her. When they captured a young servant, that case was complete. They threatened him with a beating, so he told them everything they wanted to know- and more. He told them about hiding Catholic priests. He showed them the hiding places.

On Monday 10 March 1586 they came for Margaret. She stood silent before Judge Clinch. "Have you anything to say, Margaret Clitheroe?" the judge asked.

Margaret said nothing. She knew that if she answered the charges then the law would call witnesses against her. The best witnesses would be her own children. If the children didn't want to talk then they would be tortured until they betrayed their mother.

The judge nodded. "Of course, the punishment for refusing to stand trial is Death By Crushing, do you know that, Mrs Clitheroe?"

Margaret knew. She had heard about "death by crushing". The accused was laid on the ground, face up. A sharp stone, about the size of a man's fist, was placed under the back. The face was covered with a handkerchief. A heavy door was laid on the accused. Large stones were placed on the door until the accused was crushed to death.

Margaret had to choose. Did she…

1 Remain silent and face death by crushing?
2 Stand trial and have her children as witnesses against her?

Answer: Margaret stayed silent. The city sergeants were supposed to carry out the execution on the morning of March 25th. They hadn't the courage. They hired four beggars to carry out the deed. The beggars were clumsy and she died quickly. Here last words were, "Jesu! Have mercy upon me!"

The good – the Justice of the Peace

Which would you rather do:
1 live by the laws of the Tudor land?
2 break the laws of Tudor times?
3 have the job of enforcing Tudor laws?
The people who had the job of enforcing the laws were usually Justices of the Peace. (We still have them today but they don't have so much power.)

If you were a Justice of the Peace you would have to…

1 stop riots
2 look after the building of roads, bridges, jails and poorhouses
3 decide how much local workers could be paid
4 report people who didn't go to church
5 be in charge of the whipping of beggars
6 check on the local alehouses.

But your main job would be to judge cases in your local court. Would you know all of the curious laws? Try to match the law to the crime first…

LAW	CRIME
1 Archery	A. More than 3 people making trouble together.
2 Unlawful games	B. Quarrelling
3 Rescue	C. Playing bowls, cards or dice on a holy day.
4 Barratry	D. Stirring up trouble for the king or queen.
5 Inmate	E. Refusing to go to church.
6 Riot	F. Not going to regular weapons practices.
7 Recusance	G. Taking a person or an animal by force.
8 Sedition	H. Letting part of your house to someone without a job.

Answers: 1 = F 2 = C 3 = G 4 = B 5 = H 6 = A 7 = E 8 = D

Now test your teacher! Bet they can't get more than 5!

Try your own court case

Now that you know the laws you can try a few cases. If you were a judge you'd have a lot of different punishments you could deal out. On the right is a list of the punishments – on the left is a list of crimes. Can you match the punishment to the crime?

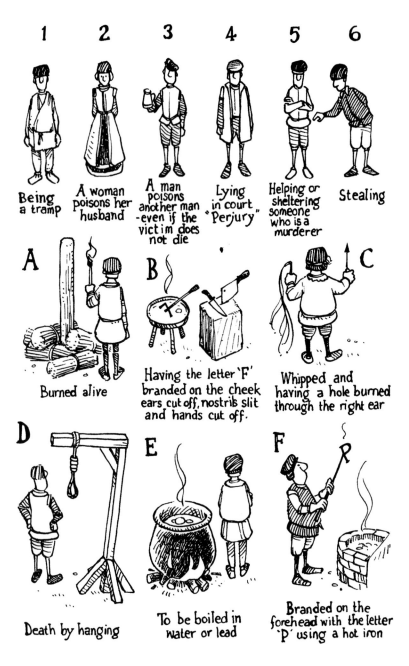

1 Being a tramp

2 A woman poisons her husband

3 A man poisons another man - even if the victim does not die

4 Lying in court "Perjury"

5 Helping or sheltering someone who is a murderer

6 Stealing

A Burned alive

B Having the letter 'F' branded on the cheek ears cut off, nostrils slit and hands cut off.

C Whipped and having a hole burned through the right ear

D Death by hanging

E To be boiled in water or lead

F Branded on the forehead with the letter 'P' using a hot iron

42

Rotten rules

There wasn't a lot of freedom in Tudor times. Henry VIII passed a law telling people how much money they could earn … a craftsman could make just six pence a day in 1514. For that you had to work from five o'clock in the morning till six o'clock at night from March to September. In the winter months you would just(!) work from sunrise till sunset with one hour for breakfast and one-and-a-half hours for lunch. A servant could earn 160 pence a year - but a woman–servant could only earn 120 pence!

Elizabeth I passed a law telling people they could only wear clothes the queen thought suitable. And you had to wear a woollen hat on Sunday - or else! (That was so the English wool trade could make big profits and pay lots of lovely taxes to the queen!)

Even if you stayed out of trouble with the Justices of the

43

Peace, you still had to worry about work. Most workers belonged to a Guild - a sort of union for their trade. There were guilds for goldsmiths and weavers and carpenters and shoemakers and so on. And every guild had its own laws. Heaven help you if you broke a guild law! It was worst for the young people who joined the guilds for the first time - the "Apprentices". Here are just a few of the rules they had to obey...

Apprentices must not use any music by night or day in the streets. Neither shall they wear their hair long, nor hair at their ears like ruffians (1603).

And the punishment for long hair? A basin was put over the boy's head and the hair chopped off in a straight line. He was then sent to prison for ten days! (We still call a straight-cut fringe a pudding-basin cut.)

Apprentices were in trouble in 1554 for *playing cards, drinking, dancing and embracing women,* and their appearance was so grand and flashy they were banned from wearing silk-lined clothes, from having beards or from carrying daggers.

In a Weaver's Guild meeting (1527) you had to behave or …
Any brother misbehaving at meetings to be fined six pounds of wax.
(Wax was valuable, as it was needed for candles)

… but worse, such was the hatred between the Scots and the English, that
Any brother calling another "Scot" to be fined six shillings and eight pence.
… that's twelve weeks' wages!

The Tudor law

The rich nobles had been a "law unto themselves" - the Tudors put a stop to that. They were no longer allowed to keep private armies.

Bribing of judges and juries had been common the Tudors stopped that … well, *mostly!*

The rich had been able to dodge the law - now rich lawbreakers could be taken before the Tudor kings' "Star Chamber". Punishments usually took the form of big fines.

Terrible Tudor detectives

The Tudors had no policemen. They did take it in turns to be "constables" and check on some of the laws. They also had local "detectives" called "cunning men", or "wizards". The village Cunning Man might use good magic to cure illnesses and tell fortunes. But he also had a use as a detective.

One of his methods of finding out a guilty person was to make a list of all the "suspects". Each suspect's name was written on a piece of paper. Each piece of paper was wrapped in a clay ball. The clay balls were dropped into a bucket of water. The one that unrolled first had the name of the guilty person on it! That's if the water didn't wash the ink off first!

The bad – the criminals

If you weren't afraid of being caught – or if you were very desperate for money and food to stay alive – you might become a criminal.

What sort would you like to be? A prigger of prancers? A dummerer? Or, maybe a ruffler?

What do you mean, you don't understand? If you're going to become a Tudor criminal you need to learn the language.

~ROGUES~ DICTIONARY

beak

beak – magistrate
boozing ken – ale house
a bung – a purse
chats – gallows
a cony – an easy victim
cove – man
couch a hogshead –
  go to sleep
draw – pick a pocket
filchman – strong pole for
  walking or hitting
a foist – a pickpocket
glaziers – eyes
greenman's – fields

walking mort

ken – house
lift – rob a shop
mort – woman
nab – head
peck – food
prancer – horse
prig – steal
a snap – a share of loot
stamps – legs
stow you – shut up
three trees with a ladder
  – gallows
walking mort – woman
  tramp

THAT HISTORY TEACHER'S A WALKING MORT. I WISH SHE'D STOW HER SO I CAN COUCH A HOGSHEAD. IN FACT IF YOU KEEP YOUR GLAZIERS ON HER I MAY JUST PRIG A NAP!

Become a terrible criminal!

Learn some of the language yourself – add new words of your own – and baffle everyone around you! Once you've grasped the language, you are almost ready to learn some tricks of the trade. But first you'll need a name – to protect your true identity. You need to change your name.

In Tudor times a few villains' nick-names were …
Olli Compoli,
Dimber Damber, Black Will,
Shagbag.

Women were …
the White Ewe,
the Lamb, and so on.

What would you call yourself? You can make up your own name.

The Wickedness – the crimes

What villainy would you like to be involved in? You could try being one of these…

An Autem Mort – a woman who steals clothes off washing lines.

A Hooker (or Angler) – a thief who uses a long pole with a hook on the end to "lift" other people's property.

They carry with them a staff five or six feet long, in which, within one inch of the top, is a little hole bored. In this hole they put an iron hook. With the same they will pluck unto them anything that they may reach. The hook, in the daytime, they hide and is never taken out until they come to the place where they do their stealing. They will lean upon their staff to hide the hole while they talk to you.

A Prigger of Prancers - a horse stealer.

A Ruffler- a beggar who tries to squeeze money out of you with a sad story about how he fought and was wounded in the wars.

A Dummerer- a beggar who tries to win sympathy by acting both deaf and dumb.

An Abram Man - a beggar who pretends to be mad, wears ragged clothes, dances around and talks nonsense... Try saying, "Please let me have some of your sheep's feathers to make a bed!"

Highway Robber- seems to be a beggar when he stops you on a quiet road, but when you take your purse out he snatches it and may throw you off your horse and take that too.

Palliard – a beggar with dreadful sores. Could be genuine disease, but (more often) they'd be faked.

They take crowfoot, spearwort and salt and lay them upon the part of the body they desire to make sore. The skin by this means being irritated, they first clasp to a linen cloth till it sticks fast. When the cloth is plucked off the raw flesh has rat poison thrown upon it to make it look ugly. They then cast over that a cloth which is always bloody and filthy. They do this so often that in the end they feel no pain, nor do they want to have it healed. They travel from fair to fair and from market to market. They are able to live by begging and sometimes have about them five or six pounds altogether.

A Doxy (or walking Mort) – a woman tramp.

On her back she carries a great pack in which she has all the things she steals. Her skill sometimes is to tell fortunes or to help cure the diseases of women and children. As she walks she knits and wears in her hat a needle with a thread in it. If any poultry be near she feeds them with bread on the hook and has the thread tied to the hook. The chicken, swallowing this, is choked and hidden under the cloak. Chickens, clothing or anything that is worth the catching comes into her net.

50

A Cutpurse - purses were small coin-bags hanging from the belt. If you couldn't "foist" the purse (dip in and pick the money out) then you would have to "nip" it (cut the purse off).

A good foist must have three qualities that a good surgeon should have and they are an eagle's eye (to spy out where the bung lies) a lady's hand (to be little and nimble) and a lion's heart.

Terrible Shakespeare

Terrible Shakespeare has been torturing school pupils for hundreds of years!

It isn't his fault, though. Teachers were taught by teachers who were taught by teachers who were taught, "Shakespeare is the greatest poet and playwright ever. You are going to listen to him even if it bores the knickers off you! Now, sit still and stop yawning!"

In fact, Shakespeare didn't write for school pupils to read his plays and study every last word. He wrote the plays to be **acted** and **enjoyed** ... so act them and **enjoy** them.

You can start by practising a few Terrible Shakespeare insults. Go up to the nearest nasty teacher (or policeman or parent or priest) and try one of these insults on them. Then, just before they mince you into hamster food, say, "Oh, but Sir (or Miss or Constable or Your Holiness), I was just practising my Shakespeare. He's the greatest poet and playwright ever." Smile sweetly and add, "And you do want me to study Shakespeare, don't you?"

Here goes...

(Never mind what they mean … just enjoy saying them aloud!) Feeling really brave now, are you? Then try…

Feeling suicidal? Then go up to the man with the biggest ears you can find and say Shakespeare's nastiest insult…

The Tudor Theatre

Being an actor in Tudor times was just a little different from today. For a start there were no actresses in Tudor theatre. All the women's parts were played by boys. Often the women in Shakespeare's plays disguised themselves as boys, so you'd have a boy pretending to be a woman pretending to be a boy. Nowadays women play the women's parts so you have women pretending to be boys pretending to be women pretending to be boys!

Get it? Oh, never mind.

Shakespeare's theatres were all open air stages. The audience would sit around three sides of the stage - if you were poor you would have to stand … and Shakespeare's play, Hamlet, went on for over three hours!

His plays are often performed on Elizabethan style stages today. You can see them in Shakespeare's birthplace, Stratford-upon-Avon.

Most of the audience couldn't read so it was no use putting up posters. The signal that a play was going to start was a cannon fired from the top of the theatre roof. Unfortunately, one such cannon shot set fire to the thatched roof of one of Shakespeare's theatres and burned it to the ground.

Dramatic facts about William Shakespeare

1 Shakespeare was born on St. George's Day (23 April) in 1564. He died in 1616... on 23 April, St. George's day! That must have put a bit of a damper on his 52nd birthday party.

2 Shakespeare chose the epitaph for his own gravestone. It says

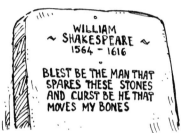

Some people think there may be new and priceless Shakespeare plays buried in the tomb ... but no one has risked the curse of digging it up.

3 In his will he left his wife his *second-best bed, with the furniture.*

4 Some people have tried to rewrite Shakespeare's plays. In the eighteenth century, a man called Nahum Tate rewrote many. He took the sad and gory tragedies (like *Macbeth*) and gave them happy endings just because people prefer them!

5 Actors are very superstitious people. Their greatest superstition is that *Macbeth* is an unlucky play. Never, never say a line from the play (unless you are acting, it of course). Don't even say the title ... call it "The Scottish Play" if you have to call it anything. And if you do act in it then watch out

... the "Macbeth Curse" may get you. This is the terrible bad luck that seems to happen to every production accident, illness and even death. Many actors will swear that it's true because it's happened to someone they know.

6 The most dramatic fact of all? Perhaps William Shakespeare didn't write William Shakespeare's plays! Some very serious teachers believe that the man called Shakespeare could not have written plays. Why not? Because...

a William Shakespeare's father could not read or write, nor could Shakespeare's children

b the few signatures of Shakespeare that remain show a very poor scrawl

c William Shakespeare was known in Stratford as a businessman, not a writer

d there are no manuscripts of Shakespeare's- plays in the man's own handwriting- there are lots from other writers of the time

e he left no manuscripts in his will and no copies of his plays are mentioned as being in his house

f a monument put up in Stratford church 15 years after he died show his hands resting on a sack (a sign of a tradesman) not a pen

g there is no evidence, apart from the name, to link the Stratford actor/businessman with the playwright.

7 Professor Calvin Hoffman has studied the language used by writers. If you look at the way a writer uses words of a certain number of letters then you can recognise his writing. Every writer is different - just as everyone has different fingerprints. Yet Shakespeare's writing "fingerprint" is

identical to that of another leading Elizabethan playwright, Christopher Marlowe.

So, did Marlowe write the plays and put William Shakespeare's name on them? Is it possible? No. Because, six months before Shakespeare's first publication, Christopher Marlowe is said to have been murdered.

Or was he...

Terrible Tudor mystery

The murder of Christopher Marlowe?

The murderer's story

Date: Wednesday 30 May 1593
Place: Eleanor Bull's Tavern, Deptford, London

Mrs Bull mopped at the spilt ale on the table with a dirty cloth. It dribbled onto the sawdust on the floor. Suddenly, three men clattered down the stairs and fell into the room. Three of the men she'd let the upstairs room to.

"Mrs Bull! Oh, Mrs Bull!" the skinny Ingram Frizer gasped as he clutched at his head.

"What's wrong?" the woman snapped. Frizer was a well-known trickster who'd tried to cheat her more than once.

The man took his hand away from his head. It was soaked in blood. "Murder!" he said hoarsely.

"Sit down," she said briskly. Frizer's two friends, Skeres and Poley, helped him to a bench. The woman mopped at the head wounds with her ale cloth and sniffed. "Not murder, Mr Frizer, just a couple of two inch cuts. You'll not die. Who did it?"

"Marlowe," the man moaned, "Christopher Marlowe."

The woman looked at the stairs and snatched a bread knife from the bar. "Roaming around stabbing people, is he?"

The wounded man shook his head slowly. "Not any more, he's not."

Mrs Bull relaxed. "You overpowered him, then?"

Frizer's voice dropped to a whisper. "I killed him!"

The landlady grabbed the man by the collar and marched him towards the stairs. "Let's have a look at poor Mr Marlowe, shall we?" she demanded. Frizer couldn't argue. Skeres and Poley lurked behind as she threw open the door.

The body lay on the floor. One lifeless eye stared at the ceiling. The other was covered in blood from a neat wound just above it.

"I knew you were trouble, you three," the woman moaned. aThat Mr Marlowe seemed such a nice young man. What happened?" She looked closely at the body and shook her head. "Doesn't look a bad enough wound to kill a man that quick," she muttered.

Frizer swayed and let himself fall onto the bed.

"He was lying here, on this bed. We had our backs to him, didn't we Poley?"

Poley nodded. The local men said Poley made his money from spying. "Our backs to him," he said.

"Suddenly he jumped up from the bed, snatched my dagger and started stabbing at my head!" Frizer groaned. "I had Skeres on one side of me and Poley on the other. I couldn't get out of the way, could I?"

"He couldn't!" Skeres agreed. Everybody knew that Skeres was a cutpurse and a robber.

"If he attacked you from behind he could have killed you easily, not just scratched your scalp, Mr Frizer," the landlady argued.

"I moved," the man said lamely.

"Then he stabbed himself in the eye, did he?" Mrs Bull asked with a sneer.

"No!" Poley cried. "I managed to get the dagger from

him. We struggled. It went into his eye by accident."

"A strange sort of accident. Doesn't look the sort of wound you'd get from a scuffle. Looks more like he was lying on his back when the knife went in," the woman said carefully.

The three men looked at each other nervously.

"Just one of those things," Poley mumbled.

"So what were you arguing about?" the landlady asked. "I didn't hear any argument."

"About the bill," Frizer said quickly.

"And why didn't your two friends help?" she asked suspiciously.

"It wasn't our argument," Skeres shrugged.

"You'll hang for this, Mr Frizer," Mrs Bull said contentedly.

Frizer looked up slowly from the bed. A curious smile came over his face. "Oh no I won't, Mrs Bull. Oh, no I won't."

And he didn't.

A strange sort of accident indeed. But the jury decided that was just what it was. You might have decided the same if you'd been on the jury. But looking back over 400 years you have a few more facts to go on. Here they are...

The powerful and important Sir Thomas Walsingham was a friend of all of the men and could have helped them get away with a plan such as this. Christopher Marlowe was certainly his closest friend.

Marlowe was in deep trouble at the time of his "death". His friend, Thomas Kyd, had just been arrested for having writings which said that Jesus was not the Son of God. The punishment for this was death. Kyd said the writings belonged to Christopher Marlowe! (It did Kyd no good - he died after being "put to torture" in prison a year later.)

Frizer went back to work for Walsingham after he had been tried for the murder of Marlowe.

So what happened in Mrs Bull's tavern that day? If you don't believe Frizer's story, here are two other stories that fit the facts…

The execution theory

Marlowe had been careless. He'd left those writings in Kyd's room. Marlowe would be arrested and executed. Marlowe was as good as dead.

Kyd had accused Marlowe. But if Marlowe went to court he might have brought Sir Thomas Walsingham into all this. That would never have done.

Sir Thomas called his three loyal cut-throats to him. He gave them their orders, "Kill Marlowe and I will reward you well. Make it look like an accident and I'll use all my power to make sure the court lets you go free."

The three agreed to meet Marlowe in the tavern. As the playwright lay drunk on the bed, Skeres and Poley held him down while Frizer pushed the knife into his eye. Skeres or Poley then gave Frizer a couple of cuts on the head to back up their story of a fight.

Or…

The escape theory

Sir Thomas Walsingham was a great friend of Christopher Marlowe. He heard that Marlowe was about to be arrested for a crime that could lead to his execution. Sir Thomas wanted to protect his friend.

He called the four men to his house and told them of his

plan. Marlowe must leave the country as soon as possible. As soon as he was safe abroad the other three must take a stranger to Mrs Bull's tavern and kill him.

After the murder, Frizer must confess. Say it was a fight and that "Marlowe" had been killed. When a man owns up to murder, the constables are interested in establishing the killer – not the identity of the victim. The stranger was buried in a grave named "Christopher Marlowe" and the real Marlowe was safe.

Of course, the real Marlowe was a successful playwright. Imagine Marlowe wants to go on writing plays. So he does. He sends them to Walsingham. Walsingham gives them to an actor. An ambitious young man who happily signs his own name to Marlowe's plays.

He signs them, "William Shakespeare".

Possible? What do you think? Remember, history is not always simple or straightforward. In cases like this historians make up their own minds from the facts that they have. So, you can be an historical "police officer". In cases like this, what you think is as good as what another historian might think.

Terrible Tudor kings and queens

Things they try to teach you

Henry VII
Henry Tudor became King Henry VII after defeating
Richard III at the Battle of Bosworth Field.

True, but Henry had a lot of help from other lords,
including one (Stanley) who might have fought for
Richard. When he chose to fight for Henry he won
the battle for him and changed the course of English history!

Richard III was a grotesque man - he was hunch-
backed and cruel.

Richard was no crueller than most rulers of the
time. The stories of his twisted body were added to
by Henry Tudor's history writers. England was full
of cruel lords - only the cruellest of all could hope to control
them and that was Henry Tudor!

Richard III died in battle crying, 'A horse, A horse!
My kingdom for a horse!'

That's extremely unlikely! The lines were written
by William Shakespeare 100 years after the battle in
his play *Richard III*.

When Richard was killed in the Battle of Bosworth,
his crown was found hanging from a thorn-bush and
Henry was handed it on the battlefield.

It's a nice image, but not necessarily true.

Henry was fighting Richard III in the so-called 'Wars of the Roses'. Richard was fighting under the White Rose of the York Family emblem and Henry Tudor under the Red Rose of the Lancaster Family emblem.

In fact Richard fought under the banner of a Boar, while Henry Tudor battled under the Dragon symbol of his native Wales. The white-rose/red-rose idea was thought up by Henry Tudor years later.

 Henry VII was a clever man and a wise ruler.

True - but he was also a man of the Middle Ages with some strange ideas. The story goes that he'd heard that the Mastiff type of dog was the only one brave enough to attack a lion. But the symbol on the English flag was a lion - so he ordered all the Mastiff dogs in England to be destroyed! (Richard was just as superstitious. Freak weather conditions meant that there appeared to be two suns shining in the sky before the battle of Bosworth Field. Richard took this as a sign that he was going to lose . . . and he did.)

 Henry VII made England a wealthy country by carefully handling its money.

True - but Henry was so careful with money most people would call him very, very mean! And he wanted lots of money so that he didn't have to beg Parliament for it - which meant that he didn't have to take any notice of what Parliament said.

 All the money Henry VII saved for England was spent by his son, Henry VIII…

True!

Things you could try to teach them!

Henry VIII

• Henry is famous for his six wives. But, did you know that in just one year (1536) his first wife (Catherine) died, his second (Anne Boleyn) was beheaded and he married his third (Jane Seymour).

• Henry was fond of cock-fighting so he had his own cock-fighting pit built at Whitehall in London. There are different battles fought on the site today - it is number 10 Downing Street, the home of the Prime Minister!

•Henry was famous for his love of music. He composed many pieces and was a keen singer. He owned ten trombones, 14 trumpets, five bagpipes, 76 recorders and 78 flutes. It is said he composed the tune, *Greensleeves*.

• Henry was a show-off. He organised a great tournament near Calais in France, known as the *Field of the Cloth of Gold*. It seemed mainly a chance for him to display his own sporting talents. He is said to have tired out six horses while performing a thousand jumps . . . *to the delight of everyone*.

• Henry was an expert archer. He used to have competitions with a hundred of his guards and often did well. *At the Field of the Cloth of Gold* in 1520 he amazed people by hitting the bulls-eye repeatedly at a distance of 220 metres.

• Henry fancied himself as a wrestler. At a wrestling contest at the *Field of the Cloth of Gold* he created a stir by challenging King Francis I of France with the words. . . Brother we will wrestle. Francis couldn't refuse even though Henry was taller and heavier. Francis used a French-style trip and won - the English thought this was cheating; the French probably thought it served big Henry right.

• Henry liked to play an indoor tennis game called "Paume". He didn't go to see his wife, Anne Boleyn, executed. He was playing tennis while she had her head chopped off. As soon as he was brought the news of Anne's death, he rushed off to see his next love, Jane Seymour.

I'M BEING TREATED IN A VERY BACKHAND MANNER

• Even hard Henry VIII had a heart. He needed a son to carry on the Tudor royal name. He was so furious when Anne Boleyn produced baby Elizabeth that he refused to go to the christening!

• Henry wanted to get rid of Anne Boleyn for giving him only a female child. Her other babies died. One of the things he accused her of was being a witch. He had some support from the Tudor people in this. Anne had been born with a sign of the devil on her … she had six fingers on her left hand!

• Only his third wife, Jane Seymour, gave him the son he wanted - then she died a few days later. Of his six wives it was Jane Seymour he asked to be buried next to when he died.

• Henry agreed to marry Anne of Cleves after he was shown a picture of her. She turned out to be a bit uglier than the picture. Henry was so upset he accused the Dutch of sending him a horse instead of a princess. He called her the Flanders Mare and divorced her after just six months.

Elizabeth I - what they said about her

It's difficult to know what Elizabeth looked like because although there are a lot of portraits of her, she didn't pose for many of them. And if a picture displeased her then she would have it destroyed.

Many painters have done portraits of the queen but none has sufficiently shown her looks or charms. Therefore her majesty commands all manner of persons to stop doing portraits of her until a clever painter has finished one which all other painters can copy. Her majesty, in the meantime, forbids the showing of any portraits which are ugly until they are improved. Lord Cecil

So, will we ever know exactly what she looked like? Only from what people wrote about her. Could you draw her from the descriptions?

She is now about twenty-one years old; her figure and face are very handsome; she has such an air of dignified majesty that no one could ever doubt that she is a queen.

VENETIAN AMBASSADOR

She is now twenty-three years old; although her face is comely rather than handsome, she is tall and well-formed, with a good skin, although swarthy; she has fine eyes and, above all, a beautiful hand with which she makes display.

ANOTHER VENETIAN AMBASSADOR

> *Her hair was more reddish than yellow, curled naturally in appearance.*

SCOTTISH AMBASSADOR 1564

> *In her sixty-fifth year her face is oblong, fair, but wrinkled; her eyes small, yet black and pleasant; her nose a little hooked; her teeth black (a fault the English seem to suffer from because of their great use of sugar); she wore false hair, and that red; her hands were small, her fingers long and her height neither tall nor short; her air was stately, her manner of speaking mild and good-natured.*

GERMAN VISITOR 1598

> *When anyone speaks of her beauty she says she was never beautiful. Nevertheless, she speaks of her beauty as often as she can.*

de MAISSE FRENCH VISITOR 1597

Elizabeth did not want to have her rotten teeth removed. Perhaps she was afraid. To show her how easy and painless it was, the brave Bishop of London had one of his own teeth taken out while she watched.

What Elizabeth I said about herself

I know I have the body of a weak and feeble woman, but I have the heart and stomach of a king, and a king of England too. I think foul scorn that any prince of Europe shall dare to invade the borders of my realm.

SHE WOULDN'T WANT THE STOMACH OF HENRY VIII

Her speech to her troops as the Spanish Armada approached
A weak and feeble woman? That's not what writers of her time said. Elizabeth had a temper which everyone feared. William Davison, her unfortunate secretary, was just one who suffered:
She punched and kicked him and told him to get out of her sight.
And…
She threw a slipper at Walsingham (her secretary) and hit him in the face, which is not an unusual thing for her to do as she is always behaving in such a rude manner as this.
And…
Once she sent a letter to the Earl of Essex which was so fierce that he fainted. He became so swelled up that all the buttons on his doublet broke away as though they had been cut with a knife.

What can we do about Mary?

In 1568 Mary Queen of Scots had to leave Scotland in a great hurry. She was suspected of being mixed up in the murder of her husband, and she was a Catholic. She also had a claim to the throne of England. She was a threat to Elizabeth, so what could Elizabeth do?

Elizabeth kept Mary in prison for a few years while she made up her mind. (It was 16 years in all Elizabeth could sometimes take a long time to make up her mind!) Then, in 1587, Mary was proved to be plotting against Elizabeth. The English Queen had to act quickly. If you were Elizabeth I what would you do? You could…

1 help poor Mary to get her Scottish throne back: after all she is related to you through Henry VII but this would upset the Scottish Protestants and may cause a war with Scotland if the plan failed.

2 let her go abroad to Catholic France or Spain - but Mary might get those countries to join her in a war to take the English throne. The English Catholics would certainly support her.

3 hand Mary back to the Scots for trial and possible execution - but Mary is a relative.

4 execute her - but English Catholics might rebel with help from Spain and France. And could you be so cruel as to do this to a woman who came to you for help?

5 sign an order for Mary to be executed. Wait for the execution to be carried out, then try to cancel the order. When the cancellation arrives too late say, "Oh, dear! I did sign the execution order - but I never really meant it to be delivered! It's the messenger's fault! Put him in the Tower of London!" But nobody would swallow that, and Spain or France may still attack.

6 keep Mary in prison – but English, French or Spanish Catholics may try to free her.

What did Elizabeth decide? Number 5.

The Queen's mind was greatly troubled. She signed a death warrant for Mary and gave it to Davison, her secretary. The next day she changed her mind but it was too late. The warrant was delivered and Mary was executed. William Davison was fined heavily and put in the Tower of London.

According to one account, Mary was beheaded by a clumsy executioner who took at least three blows of the axe and a bit of sawing to finish the job. This eyewitness described it ...

The executioners desired her to forgive them for her death. She answered, "I forgive you with all my heart for now, I hope, you shall make an end to all my troubles."

Kneeling down upon a cushion, without any fear of death, she spoke a psalm. Then she laid down her head, putting her chin on the block. Lying very still on the block she suffered two strokes with the axe, making very little noise or none at all. And so the executioner cut off her head, sawing one little gristle. He then lifted up her head to the view of all the assembly and cried, "God save the Queen!"

Elizabeth did apologise to Mary's son, James …

My dearest brother, I want you to know the huge grief I feel for something which I did not want to happen and that I am innocent in the matter.

So that was all right!

But the Spanish didn't believe in Elizabeth's innocence – they didn't want to. King Philip II of Spain was sick of English ships raiding his own, laden with treasure from his overseas territories. Philip was a Catholic, like Mary. So he used her execution as an excuse to send a huge invasion fleet, The Armada, to take revenge for these English crimes. But that's another story …

Mary's Secret Message

Did Mary Queen of Scots deserve to die? Elizabeth had sheltered her when she fled from Scotland. How did she repay Elizabeth? By plotting with Elizabeth's enemies, especially English Catholics, to kill her. Of course Mary didn't go shouting it from the rooftops. It was a secret plot between her and the English conspirators. The leader of these treacherous plotters was a rich young Derbyshire man called Anthony Babbington.

So, if it was secret, how did Elizabeth find out about it? She found out because she had a very clever spy in her service, Sir Francis Walsingham. First, Walsingham sent servants to Mary's prison who pretended to work for Mary … in fact they were spying on her.

Every time Mary sent a letter to Babbington the servants took it to Walsingham first. Mary tried writing in code. But she had sent the code to Babbington first. Walsingham had a copy. This is Mary's code…

A	B	C	D	E	F	G	H	I	J	K	L	M
O	‡	∧	⧺	α	▢	θ	∞	ı		ŏ	∩	८

N	O	P	Q	R	S	T	U	V	W	X	Y	Z
⌀	▽	s	m	⊥	Δ	ε	c	v	w	7	8	9

OF	THE	NOT	FROM	YOU
m̲	♂	X	✕	ꝯ

And this is part of the message that Walsingham read and passed on to Queen Elizabeth - the part that led to Mary's execution. Use the code to read it.

∩αε ♂ θ⊥αoε sn▽ε θ▽ o∞αo⧺

Δıθ⌀αⅲ

८o⊥8

You could try writing your own messages in this code.

Elizabeth I's sharp and cruel tongue

It was said that if someone tall disagreed with her she would promise …

I will make you shorter by a head.

She seemed to have a thing about height. She asked a Scot how tall Mary Queen of Scots was. The man replied that Mary was taller than Elizabeth. Elizabeth said … *She is too tall, then; for I myself am neither too tall nor too short.* And, of course, Elizabeth then went on to make Mary Queen of Scots "shorter by a head"!

Elizabeth also made her favourite the Earl of Essex "shorter by a head" when he tried to lead a rebellion against her in February 1601. She was so fond of him that she wore his ring for the rest of her life. It must have upset her to order his execution … though not as much as it upset Essex.

Elizabeth's "wedding" ring

Elizabeth was the last Tudor because she never married and had children. Some people dared to hint that she should marry. Her reply was:

I have already joined myself in marriage to a husband, namely the kingdom of England.

Then she would show her coronation ring. She went on:
Do not blame me for the miserable lack of children; for everyone of you are children of mine.
But, when Elizabeth grew old and fat, the ring began to cut into her finger. She had to have it sawn off in January 1603. The superstitious Tudors saw this as a sign that her "marriage" to the country was ended. Two months later she was dead.

Not a lot of people know that …

… Elizabeth was one of the cleanest women in England. She was proud of the fact that she took a bath once every three months. One person was amazed and reported that she had four baths a year *whether she needed it or not!* (Even 100 years later King Louis XIV of France only had three baths in his whole life!)

… Elizabeth was' a fan of an early sort of five-a-side tennis …
About three o'clock, ten men hung up lines in a square grass court in front of her majesty's windows.

They squared out the form of the court making a cross line in the middle. Then in this square (having taken off their doublets) they played five on each side, with a small ball, to the great liking of her highness ...

Queen Elizabeth owned the first wristwatch in the world. Perhaps she lost it, because her dying words were ...

All my possessions for a moment of time.

Terrible Tudor joke ...

The Tudors were Henry VII, Henry VIII, Edward VI and Mary ... but who came after Mary?

Answer: Her little lamb.

Terrible Tudor witches

Black cats and broomsticks

Witches casting magic spells then flying off on their broomsticks. They make great stories. But few people believe them today. The Tudors, though, thought that witches were capable of anything. And unfortunately for the so-called witches, the Tudors believed the best way to deal with a witch was to burn him or her. (Seven out of every ten people accused of being witches were women.) Some "witches" believed they would be spared if they admitted they were witches. In 1565 Elizabeth Francis confessed…

I learnt this art of witchcraft at the age of twelve years from my grandmother. She told me to renounce God and his word and to give my blood to Satan. She gave me Satan in the form of a white spotted cat. She taught me to feed the cat with bread and milk and to call it by the name of Satan.

When I first had the cat Satan I asked it to make me rich. He promised me I should and asked what I would like (for the cat spoke to me in a strange, hollow voice.) I said, "Sheep," and this cat at once brought 18 sheep to my pasture, black and white. They stayed with me for a time, but in the end did all vanish away. I know not how.

I then asked for a husband, this Francis whom I now have, and the cat promised that I should have him. We were married and had a child but we did not live as quietly as I'd hoped. So I willed Satan to kill my six-month old child and he did.

When I still could not find a quiet life I asked it to make my husband lame. It did it in this way. It came one morning to Francis' shoe, lying in it like a toad. As he put on the shoe he touched it with his foot and he was taken with a lameness that will not heal.

Elizabeth said that she gave the cat to her friend Agnes Waterhouse. Agnes claimed that the cat ...
killed a pig
killed three of a priest's pigs
drowned a cow
drowned geese
killed a neighbour
killed her husband.

Elizabeth Francis went to prison for a year – by confessing to her witchcraft she saved her life. Agnes Waterhouse was hanged.

The truth about Margaret

If you were Margaret Harkett's judge you might decide …

1 William Goodwin hated the old woman because she was a beggar and a nuisance.

2 Goodwin's lamb must have been sick because healthy lambs aren't brought into the kitchen.

3 The lamb dying at the same time as Margaret's visit was just bad luck - coincidence.

You might also decide …

1 Mrs Frynde was upset and bitter at the death of her husband and wanted to blame someone.

2 Frynde's fall from the pear tree was bad luck.

3 It was odd that Frynde never mentioned the curse until he was dying.

4 Frynde died of one of the many illnesses of those times or as a result of the fall.

Do you judge Margaret Harkett "Guilty" or "Not Guilty"? What did her judge do in 1585?

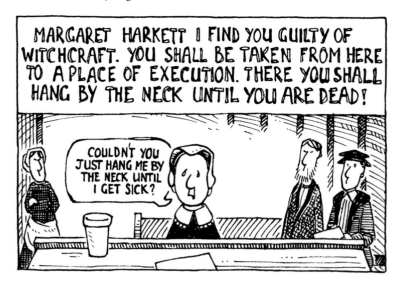

84

Margaret was executed. So were hundreds of other old women who were simply blamed for any accidents or illnesses in the area. They were usually alone – they had no one to stand up for them. They were usually too weak to stand up to their bullying neighbours.

Which is witch?

The Tudors had a way of testing a person for witchcraft. They would put the suspected witch into a sack and throw them into a nearby pond or stream. If s/he floated then s/he was a witch and would be taken out and executed. If s/he sank then s/he was innocent … but probably dead from drowning.

Another test was to have the accused witch recite the *Lord's Prayer* without one mistake – could you do that, knowing that the first slip and you would die?

Witch fact …

In the sixteenth and seventeenth centuries about 100,000 people in Europe were accused of being witches and were killed.

Witchcraft laws

Witchcraft wasn't seen as particularly serious until 1542, when it became punishable by death if it was used for ...

... discovering treasure

... injuring others

... unlawful love

In 1569 a list of magical practices that were banned included ...

... curing men or beasts

... summoning wicked spirits

... telling where things were lost

Tudor superstitions

The death rate from disease was very high in Tudor times. Babies were especially likely to die from an illness. With so much death around the Tudors tried their own type of "witchcraft" to keep death and bad luck away. They didn't call their actions "witchcraft" - they called it "superstition". Some of the things they believed may seem odd to us today. They believed ...

... when a baby was born they must ring church bells to frighten away evil spirits. Sometimes evil fairies stole the child and left a wicked fairy child in its place (a changeling).

... it was unlucky to wrap a new-born baby in new clothes, so it spent the first few hours of its life wrapped in an old cloth or in the clothes of older brothers or sisters. The baby had to be carried upstairs before it was carried downstairs.

... the twelfth night after Christmas was another time when evil spirits were flying around - protect yourself by chalking a cross on the beams of your house.

... it was unlucky if a hare ran in front of you - **hares**, they thought, were one of the shapes that a witch took to get around the country quickly! (Witches also disguised themselves as cats, dogs, rats, toads, wasps or butterflies. They would be fed with milk, bread and blood sucked from the witch.)

THAT'S NO REGULAR BUTTERFLY !!

... it was unlucky to leave empty eggshells lying about - they could become a witch's boat.

... in an ancient way to tell your fortune. You had to jump over a lighted candle. If the candle stayed lit then good luck was coming . . . but if the candle went out then bad luck was sure to follow. Which nursery rhyme describes this fortune-telling method?

Answer: *Jack be nimble, Jack be quick, Jack jump over the candlestick*

Witch ghosts

In Buxted, Sussex, there is a lane called Nan Tuck's Lane. Nan Tuck had been accused of being a witch and the villagers tried to drown her. Nan escaped but was later found hanging in a nearby wood. Her ghost can be still seen running to the safety of the church, along Nan Tuck's Lane.

It is said that the screams of witches tortured by the witch-finder general can be heard in the dead of night at Seafield Bay in Suffolk.

Anne Chattox, the head of a group of Lancashire witches, was accused of digging up three skulls from a churchyard to use in a spell. She was hanged.

Father Ambrose Barlow's skull can be seen not far away, at Wardley Hall in Lancashire. He was a Catholic priest who died for his faith. The legend goes that this skull must not be disturbed in any way... or else it will give the most blood-chilling scream you ever heard!

Terrible Tudor food

Foul facts on food

Tudor women, men and children in England drank beer, wine, sherry (or "sack"), mead and cider. This was not because they were drunkards. It was because the water was not fit to drink unless boiled.

The rich could buy or hunt for a wide range of meats. The poor had very little meat. Their main food was bread. Sometimes they caught rabbits, hares or fish to go with their turnips. beans and cabbage.

Tudor people were keen on spices. Most of the food was heavily salted to stop it going bad, so spices helped to disguise the salty taste. It also disguised the taste of rotten meat! Cinnamon, cloves, garlic and vinegar were all used.

Sugar was a rare luxury but, when they could get some, they used it on most of their food ... including meat! Their other means of sweetening food was with honey.

Hot cross buns were made at Easter- but not always eaten - they were kept as luck charms instead!

Sailors had too much salt meat and not enough fresh vegetables on their long sea journeys. As a result they developed a disease called scurvy. Their gums began to rot, their breath to smell and their teeth began to drop out. Henry VIII's ship, the *Mary Rose*, was sunk in 1545 but recovered in 1982. The sailors had drowned, but modern-day tests show that many were already dying of scurvy.

People who went to see a play would usually eat while they watched. The actors could be really put off by people cracking nuts or trampling on the shells while they tried to act!

Four-and-twenty blackbirds baked in a pie? Not so daft a rhyme. Tudors and Stuarts loved eating birds - favourites were peacocks, larks and seagulls. And not just dead birds. This incredible recipe was included in a cookery book…

TO MAKE PIES THAT THE BIRDS MAY BE ALIVE IN THEM AND FLY OUT WHEN IT IS CUT UP

Make the piecrust of a great pie.
Fill it full of flour and bake it.
Being baked, open a hole at the bottom and take out the flour.
Then having a real pie the size of the hole, put it inside the piecrust. Put under the piecrust, around the real pie, as many small live birds as the empty piecrust will hold.
This to be done before such a time as you send the pie to the table and set it before the guests
Uncovering, or cutting up the great lid of the pie, all the birds will fly out, which is a delight and a pleasure to the guests.
So that they may not be hungry, you shall cut open the small pie.

ye woman's weekly pg 76

Got that? A big, **fake** piecrust covers a small, **real** pie **and** a flock of birds, yes? But the recipe doesn't explain what the birds are doing to the small pie - or what they are doing on the small pie - while they are waiting to be released.

Tudor foods you may want to eat

EGGS IN MUSTARD SAUCE

Ingredients:
Eggs - one for each person
& for each egg -
25 g butter
5 ml mustard (1 teaspoon)
5 ml vinegar (1 teaspoon)
A pinch of salt

Cooking:
Boil the eggs for 5 to 6 minutes.
While the eggs are boiling put the butter in a small saucepan and heat it.
When the butter has melted and begins to turn brown, take it off the heat.
Stir in the salt, mustard and vinegar.
When the eggs are ready remove the shells, cut them into quarters and put them on a warm dish.
Heat up the sauce again and pour it over the eggs.

ye womans weekly pg 77

JUMBLES (KNOTTED BISCUITS)
Ingredients:

2 eggs   15 ml aniseed or caraway (3 teasp)
100 sugar   175g plain flour

Cooking :

Beat the eggs. Add the sugar and aniseed
(or caraway) and beat again. Stir in the flour
to make a thick dough. Knead the dough on a
floured board. Make the dough into rolls 1cm
wide by 10cm long. Tie the strips into a single
knot. Drop the knotted dough (6 at a time)
into a pan of boiling water. They will sink to
the bottom so use a spoon after a minute to help
them float to the top. When the knots have floated
for a minute and swelled, take them out of the
water and let them drain on a wire rack. Put the
knots on buttered baking sheets and bake for
15 minutes at Gas Mark 4 (or 350 degrees F. or
180 degrees C.). Turn them over and bake for
another 10 minutes until they are golden brown.

A Tudor guide to table manners

Do you ever get nagged for your behaviour at the dinner table? So did Tudor children. These complaints may sound familiar. A 1577 Tudor book suggested ...

At the table you must ... not make faces
Scratch not thy head with thy fingers when thou art at meat.
not shout
Fill not thy mouth too full, lest thou perhaps must speak.
not gulp down drink too fast
Pick not thy teeth with thy knife nor with thy finger end.
not shuffle feet not blow on food to cool it
Nor blow out thy crumbs when thou dost eat.
not take all the best food for yourself
Foul not the place with spitting where thou dost sit.

Terrible Tudor greed

The rich would eat much more than the poor. One feast for Henry VIII at Greenwich Palace lasted seven hours. Breakfast for the poor would be boringly the same every day - bread and ale; sometimes porridge made with peas or beans.

The tables of the rich would be laid with the usual salt, bread, napkins, spoons and cups. But each guest used his or her own knife.

And where were the plates? They used large slabs of bread called "trenchers" instead. The food was served straight onto that.

Every type of fish, meat and pastry was eaten, along with 20 types of jelly. The jellies were made into the shapes of castles and animals of various descriptions.

In November 1531, Henry had five banquets at which he and his guests ate…

24 beefs
100 fat muttons
51 great veals
34 porks
91 pigs
over 700 cocks and hens
444 pigeons
168 swans
over 4000 larks.

YOU SHOULD HAVE SEEN YESTERDAY'S BREAKFAST

Many dishes were more for show than eating. A peacock would be skinned, roasted, then put back into its skin for serving. A "cockatrice" would be made by sewing the front half of a cockerel onto the back half of a baby pig before roasting.

Terrible Tudor fun and games

Blood sports

In the Middle Ages people worked long hours, but they had as much as one day in three as a holy day (a saint's day usually) or holiday. What did they do?

And what did they do on those long dark winter nights? No television or radio or records or cinema. They played sports, played games and watched sports. Some are quite similar to today's. Others are very, very different!

Animal torture

In Southwark, London, there are two bear gardens with bears, bulls and other beasts to be baited in a plot of ground for the beholders to stand safe.

A 1599 report described this "sport" …
Every Sunday and Wednesday in London there are bear baitings. The bear pit is circular with stands around the top for spectators. The ground space down below is empty.

Here a large bear on a rope was tied to a stake. Then a number of great English Mastiff dogs were brought in and shown to the bear.

After this they baited the bear, one after the other. Although the dogs were struck and mauled by the bear they d id not give in. They had to be pulled off by sheer force and their mouths forced open with long sticks. The bear's teeth were not sharp and they could not injure the dogs; they have them broken short.

When the first mastiffs tired, fresh ones were brought in to bait the bear. When the bear was tired a powerful white bull was then brought in. One dog at a time was set on him. He speared these with his horns and tossed them so they could not get the better of him. And, as the dogs fell to the floor again, several men held sticks under them to break their fall. Lastly they brought in an old, blind bear which boys hit with canes and sticks. But he knew how to untie his lead, and he ran back to his stall.

The audience might bet on which one would win.

In Congleton, Cheshire, the town had its own bear. The bear died in 1601. There is a story that the Corporation wanted a new one but didn't have the money . . . so they ordered the town bible to be sold to pay for it!

Football

Rules:
The pitch - could be the land between one village and the next - even if it is several miles. The ball - a pig's bladder or a ball of rags. Scoring - the team that gets the ball back to their village is the winner. Referee - none. Playing rules - none. Get the ball any way you can.

Match Commentary ...
Doesn't every player in a football game lie in wait for his opponent, seeking to knock him down or punch him on the nose? Sometimes the players' necks are broken, sometimes their backs, sometimes their arms and legs are thrust out of joint, and sometimes their noses gush with blood.

Hunting for fish

The rich used to hunt for small animals using trained hawks. But there was also a sport of using birds to hunt for fish. First a cormorant, a diving sea bird, was trained to come back to its owner. When it was trained its head was covered with a mask and it was taken to the sea. At the sea shore it was unmasked and allowed to fly over the sea with a leather band around its neck. When it caught a fish it would return to the owner… but the poor bird couldn't swallow the fish because the leather band was fastened too tight. The owner simply took the fish from the poor cormorant's beak!

Public executions

Very popular. The person to be executed would always dress in their finest clothes and make a speech so the spectators felt they had been to a good "show".

Play it yourself
Stoolball (Tudor Cricket)

1 Pitch two posts about four metres apart.
2 Use a bundle of rags for a ball.
3 Use a stick as a bat.

The bowler tries to stand at one post and hit the other post with the ball, while the batter tries to hit the ball. If the bowler hits the post then the batter is "out" and the next member of the team has a turn. If the batter hits the ball to a fielder he can be caught out.

The batter scores by hitting the ball and running from post to post and back again. The team that scores the most runs is the winner.

Loggats

Plant a stick in the ground, a "stake". Each player takes turns in throwing smaller sticks, "loggats". The player whose "loggat" finishes nearest the "stake" is the winner. You can invent your own scoring system.

Tame games

Table games

Dice, cards, dominoes, backgammon, chess and draughts were popular in Tudor times as they are today.

Here are some Tudor games you can try for yourself...

Hazard

You need two dice and any number of players.

1 Everyone throws two dice. The highest scorer is the "Caster".

2 The Caster throws until s/he gets 5, 6, 7, 8 or 9. The number s/he gets is the "Main Point".

3 The Caster throws again until s/he gets a number 4, 5, 6, 7, 8, 9 or 10. This is the "Chance Point". The "Chance Point" cannot be the same as the "Main Point".

4 The Caster throws again and tries to get the Chance Point - if s/he does then s/he is the winner.

5 If the Caster throws the "Main Point" before s/he manages to throw another "Chance Point" then s/he loses.

6 Use matchsticks to gamble with. If the Caster wins, s/he takes one matchstick from each player. If the Caster loses then s/he pays out a matchstick to each other player.

7 Once the Caster loses s/he passes the dice to the next player who throws for a new "Main Point" and a new "Chance Point".

Trump

You need a pack of playing cards and two or more players.

1 Place a pack of cards on the table face down.

2 Turn one card over. That number card is the "Trump".

3 Each person, one at a time, will turn the other cards over.

4 Every time one matches the "Trump", all the players hit the table with the left hand and shout "Trump!" Whoever is the last to shout and hit the table is out.

Merelles

You need a board marked like the one on page 101. Draw it onto a large piece of card.

You need ten counters, or coins, and two players.

1 Each player takes turns to place a counter on a dot.

2 The aim is to place three counters in a row.

3 If all the counters are on the board and there are no rows of three then the players can begin to move their counters.

4 A player can only move to an open dot and only one space each turn.

5 The first to get a row of three is the winner.

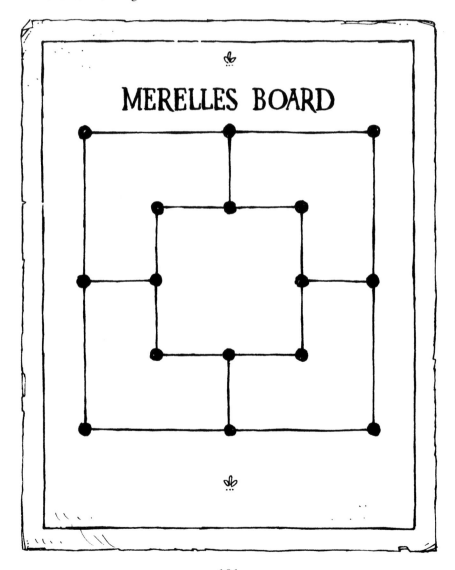

MERELLES BOARD

Some Tudor games you shouldn't play

Cudgelling

A game for two players.
1 Each is armed with a short stick.
2 The aim is to hit your opponent over the head.
3 A point is scored every time you make your opponent's head bleed!

Dun the cart-horse

A game for two equal teams.
1 The dun is a large log of wood, dragged to the centre of the village green and set upright.
2 The two teams start at opposite sides of the green. When one player shouts, "the dun is stuck in the mire," everyone rushes forward and tries to push the log over - while the other team is trying to push it over towards you.
The winning team is the one that succeeds.
But, beware! Anyone hit over the head with the log is said to be "Out" - not surprising, really!

Hurling

A game for two teams of 15 to 30 players.

1 A wooden ball is boiled in candle-grease to make it more slippery.

2 The aim is to pick up the ball and run through the other team's "goal".

3 If a player with the ball is tackled, he must pass the ball but he can only pass it backwards.

4 If your team don't have the ball then your aim is to stop the other team scoring – stop them any way you can!

Tudor sports reports

The Prior of Bicester Abbey has been paying money to players who play football on holidays. They are England's first professional footballers.

1491. Golf has been banned in Scotland by law because it's a wasteful pastime.
In no place in the country shall there be football, golf or other such unprofitable sports.

1513. King Henry VIII is so keen on bowling at Skittles that he took a portable bowling alley with him on a trip to France.

TUDOR SPORT

Terrible Tudor sailors

The sailors of Tudor Times are legendary for their daring exploits - trips around the earth in little leaking boats, fighting the mighty Spanish, French and Dutch navies, roaming the oceans with piratical plots.

Sir Francis Drake was the scourge of the oceans. He raided the coasts of the Caribbean and South America, sucking the wealth from these Spanish territories. As Drake filled Queen Elizabeth's coffers with plundered gold, she gave him more and more little jobs to do, such as helping to defeat the great Spanish Armada in 1588. It is of no surprise that many legends have been woven round Drake's cunning exploits. And wherever there are legends there are lies. Could you sort out the historical from the hysterical?

Hearing and believing

Drake's Drum

From 1577 till 1580 Sir Francis Drake sailed around the world in the service of Elizabeth I. At last, in the West Indies in 1596, he lay dying. He sent for his drum, an instrument that his men believed had magical powers. He ordered that it be sent back to England. He swore that he would return to defend his homeland if anyone beat the drum when England was in danger.

The drum was taken back to Buckland Abbey near Plymouth, where it remains to this day. The legend has changed a little over the years. The drum beats out its own warning when the country is in danger.

The drum is said to have rattled when Napoleon Bonaparte was brought to Plymouth after the battle of Waterloo. It seemed to know that the great enemy of England was nearby.

Then it has been heard three times this century. It sounded in 1914 when the first World War started; it sounded towards the end of that war when it had been taken on board the Royal Navy flagship, *The Royal Oak*.

When it sounded on *The Royal Oak*, the German fleet were approaching. They were heading towards the British fleet in order to surrender … perhaps it was giving a "Victory" salute.

Men were sent twice to find out where the noise of the drum was coming from – and twice they returned with no answer. The commander searched the ship for himself … and found nothing. Every sailor was at battle-stations in the ship. No one could have played the drum. *The Royal Oak* dropped anchor.

The drum-roll stopped as mysteriously as it had started.

The last time the drum was heard was in the darkest hours of World War Two. The British forces had crossed the channel to attack Hitler's German army. They were being driven back to the beaches. The German army was closing in, ready to massacre them. A miracle was needed.

The drum was heard sounding - the miracle occurred! A fleet of little British boats set off from the fishing ports and coastal towns of Eastern England. Somehow they crossed the channel, rescued huge numbers of men, then brought them safely home.

Was Sir Francis Drake watching over this feat of sea bravery, which was surely as great as his own trip round the world?

The Spanish Armada - Who won? Who lost?
The Spanish Armada, its special date
Is fifteen hundred and eighty-eight.

King Philip II of Spain was fed up with the English. His wife had been Mary I, Queen of England. He reckoned that he should be king, now that she was dead. But Elizabeth had grabbed the throne.
Also, English sailors were roaming the high seas and attacking the Spanish ships and colonies for their riches.

 Why was the Spanish Armada so expensive to run?

Because they only got 20 miles to the galleon.

Worse, Philip was Catholic and Elizabeth I was a Protestant, chopping off Catholic heads. In 1587 she had Mary Queen of Scots executed. This was the last straw as far as Philip was concerned.

So, in 1588 he decided it was time to teach the English a lesson once and for all. He assembled a huge fleet, an "Armada" of 130 galleons, and sent his armies off to invade England. They failed. This is what happened...

5 THE SPANISH FLEET SAILED UP THE ENGLISH CHANNEL

KEEP TOGETHER LADS, STRAIGHT LINE AT THE SPEED OF THE SLOWEST VESSEL

THEY WERE SITTING DUCKS FOR THE SMALLER FASTER ENGLISH SHIPS 6

SITTING DUCKS — OR DO I MEAN SITTING DRAKES

7 BUT THE ENGLISH DIDN'T DARE GET TOO CLOSE TO THE HUGE SPANISH GUNS

HA! YOU SANK JUST TWO SHIPS! WATER OFF A SITTING-DUCKS BACK!

8 THE SPANISH REACHED CALAIS FAIRLY SAFELY...

CALAIS

NOW I'VE GOT THEM! REMEMBER CADIZ?

9 THE ENGLISH ATTACKED THE SPANISH SHIPS WITH FIREBOATS. THEY WERE TRAPPED IN THE HARBOUR

CURSES! WHAT SHALL WE DO?

PANIC, CAPTAIN!

10 THE SPANISH PANICKED AND BLUNDERED ABOUT

ANOTHER 14 GONE ONLY 114 TO GO!

Of 130 galleons that left Spain in the summer of 1588, only about 50 returned in late September. As many as 19,000 Spaniards are thought to have died - it took them so long to sail back to Spain that many who didn't drown starved instead.

But the English sailors had their problems, too. In August 1588 the English Admiral, Lord Howard, wrote ...

The sailors cry out for money and know not when they are to be paid. I have given them my word and honour that I will see them paid. If I had not done so they would have run away from Plymouth in their thousands.

But worse was to follow. Just the next day, Howard was writing . . .

Sickness and death begin to wonderfully grow among us. It is a most pitiful sight to see, here at Margate, how the men, having no place to go, die in the streets. It would grieve any man's heart to see them that have served so bravely to die so miserably.

So, Elizabeth won - she kept her throne. But who really lost? The English sailors? The Spanish sailors? Or both?

Sir Walter Raleigh

Sir Walter Raleigh was a sailor, too … **and** a writer, **and** explorer. He was a favourite of Queen Elizabeth I. A lot of stories have been told about him … but are they all true?

Try these questions on your teacher. All they have to answer is 'True" or "False".

1 Walter Raleigh once spread his cloak in the mud for Queen Elizabeth to walk over.
True or False?

2 Walter Raleigh was the first man to bring potatoes to England. *True or False?*

3 Walter Raleigh was the first man to bring tobacco to England. *True or False?*

Answer: All are false!

110

The Truth About Walter

1 Most people have heard the story of Sir Walter Raleigh and the cloak. It was supposed to have happened when Raleigh was a young man. The queen was passing through crowds of her people when she reached a muddy puddle in the road. She stopped. After all, she didn't want to spoil her fine shoes.

Quick-thinking Walter Raleigh pulled off his new cloak and covered the puddle so she could step over without walking through mud. The queen smiled. Walter's act was to make him a rich and powerful favourite of the queen.

A great story. But a true story? No. It originated with Thomas Fuller who was a historian of the 17th century who liked to "dress up" boring history with lively little incidents like the story of Raleigh's cloak ... even if they didn't really happen!

2 Walter Raleigh's potatoes? For hundreds of years Walter Raleigh teachers have taught that Raleigh brought the first potatoes to England when he returned from a voyage to America in 1586. But there is no evidence from Tudor times to say this happened. A book called *Herball* (written by John Gerard in 1597) talks about someone called Clusius who had grown potatoes in Italy in 1585. The vegetable became very popular and was grown everywhere in Europe within ten years.

3 Walter Raleigh's tobacco? Again there are records of tobacco being used in France in 1560 - 26 years before Raleigh's ships returned from Virginia. It was brought there by John Nicot (whose name gives us "Nicotine"). It must have crossed the English Channel long before Raleigh's ships even set off.

In 1573 William Harrison wrote ...

In these days the taking in of the Indian herb called "Tobacco" is greatly taken up in England. It is used against rheums and other diseases of the lungs with great effect.

But not everyone agreed. In 1614, Barnaby Rich was writing ...

They say tobacco is good for a cold, rheums, for aches, for dropsies and for all manner of diseases. But I see the ones who smoke most are as affected by those diseases as much as the ones who don't. It is now sold in every tauern, inn and ale-house as much as beer.

Oddly enough, the man who hated tobacco smoking the most was King James I. He wrote that smoking was ...

A custom loathsome to the eye, hateful to the nose, harmful to the brain and dangerous to the lungs.

(If Raleigh really **did** smoke and James I was the first anti-smoking campaigner, then James was a great success. In 1618 he cured Raleigh's "loathsome" habit for good. James had Raleigh's head cut off for treason!)

What is it?

Drake found some new foods on his journey round the world. But what were they?

1 *We found a plant with a fruit as big as a man's head. Having taken off the back (which is full of string) you shall come to a hard shell which holds a pint of sweet liquid. Within that shell you will find a white, hard substance as sweet as almonds and half an inch thick.*

2 *We found a store of great fowl which could not fly, the bigness of geese, whereof we killed 3000 in less than one day.*

Answers: 1 Coconuts, 2 Turkeys

113

Terrible Tudor clothes

Did you know?

It was during the Tudor period that English clothes for the rich became exciting and different. Merchants were in touch with countries as far away as Russia and America. While the Tudor poor still wore rough woollen clothes, the Tudor rich were better dressed than ever before with velvets and satins from Italy, lace from France and starch from Holland. And starch meant they could make those stiff collars, "Ruffs", that were so popular in Elizabeth's time. But …

Ten things you probably didn't know …

1 Sometimes the stiff ruffs were so wide that ladies couldn't reach their mouths to eat! Silversmiths had to make extra-long spoons for them.

2 Ruffs were usually white but could be another colour. Yellow ruffs were popular for a while. Then a famous murderess, Mrs Turner, was hanged wearing one. They suddenly went out of fashion!

3 A puritan, Philip Stubbes, claimed …

The devil invented these great ruffs. But if it happen that a shower of rain catch them, then their great ruffs fall, as dishcloths fluttering in the wind.

4 Henry VIII looks very fat in his portraits. But as well as having an over-fed body, his clothes were thick with padding- at least it kept him warm in his draughty castles.

5 The Elizabethan ladies' fashion was for tiny waists. To help them squeeze into smart dresses, the ladies (and even the girls) wore iron corsets.

6 Girls showed that they were unmarried by wearing no hat in public.

7 Elizabethan men wore short trousers called "hose". They had to pad them so they wouldn't show any creases. They weren't too fussy what they padded them with - horsehair (itchy!), rags or even bran (horsefood)! If the "hose" split the bran would run

8 Poor country girls often wore shoes with iron rings under them. Sometimes they had thick wooden soles. This was to keep their skirts out of the deep mud and rubbish in the streets and market places.

  EARLY PLATFORMS

9 In 1571, Elizabeth's parliament made a law forcing all married women to wear white knitted caps, and all men (over the age of six) to wear woollen hats. The caps and hats had to be knitted in England using English wool. Elizabeth got a lot of taxes from the wool trade – English wool was in great demand from other countries, too.

10 Aprons were quite a new idea in Tudor times. You could often tell a man's occupation from the design of his apron . . .

millers and cooks   – white
barbers   – checked
builders and blacksmiths   – leather

Terrible Tudor trousers

If you'd like to act like a Tudor, feel like a Tudor, or if you're off to a fancy dress party, you may like to try making these Tudor "hose".

1 Wear a pair of tights or tight trousers first.

2 Take a pair of old, baggy trousers. Cut them off at the knee. Slit them as shown.

3 Put the baggy trousers on over the tights. Tie them at the knee with ribbon or a scarf.

4 Stuff the baggy trousers with material of a different colour so it shows through the slits.

5 Wear a loose shirt and ruff and a belt with a sword or dagger - wooden, of course.

6 Go around saying, *To be or not to be, or Alas, poor Yorick.* (They're famous lines from William Shakespeare plays – adults and teachers will be totally impressed.)

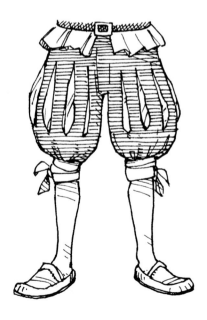

A ruff idea

1 Take seven 24 cm doilies (lacey paper table decorations, usually used at parties).

2 Cut them in half.

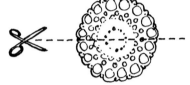

Use sticky tape to attach them to a 4 m strip of ribbon, allowing enough ribbon to tie at the back.

3 Make 2 cm folds in the doilies folding each one into a fan shape.

4 Keep the folds in place at the ribbon end with small stitches or sticky tape.

5 Tie the ends of the ribbon around your neck.

6 Wear with a collarless shirt (boys). Girls, wear with a blouse and full-length skirt.

7 Stroll around singing *Greensleeves*.

Terrible Tudor life for women

A woman's life is hard in ten terrible ways ...

1 Girls could marry at 12 (boys at 14). This was usually arranged by their parents. They would still live with their parents at this age, though.

2 Many upper-class girls were married by 15. At the age of 16 they could live with their husbands.

3 It wasn't usually considered worth the money to send a girl to school. Her mother could teach her all the household crafts she would need to be a useful wife.

4 If a girl didn't marry there wasn't much she could do. The convents had been abolished by Henry VIII so she couldn't become a nun. Very often, unmarried girls would have to stay at home with their parents and spin. That's why they became known as "spinsters" - a word we still use.

JUST BECAUSE I DIDN'T GET MARRIED WHEN I WAS STILL PLAYING WITH MY TEDDY MEANS I'VE GOT TO SIT AND SPIN FOR THE REST OF MY LIFE

5 One farmer described a good wife's behaviour. He said she should …

pray when first getting out of bed, then clean the house, lay the table, milk the cows, dress her children, cook meals for the household, brew and bake when needed, send corn to the mill, make butter and cheese, look after the swine and collect the eggs.

6 Anthony Fitzherbert added to that list and said she should …

shear corn and in time of need help her husband to fill the dung cart, drive the plough, load hay and go to market to sell butter, cheese, milk, eggs, chickens, pigs, geese and all manner of corn. (What did he expect her to do in her spare time?!)

7 But English women were better off than those in other countries - at least, that's what the men said! Thomas Platter said that …

the womenfolk of England have more freedom than in any other land. The men must put up with such ways and may not punish them for it. Indeed, the good wives often beat the men.

8 Girls were expected to help in the house by collecting fine feathers (down) for mattresses, making candles, spinning, weaving and embroidering. Once every three months, the household tablecloths and bed-clothes were washed; the girls were expected to help with this.

9 Women could be punished for nagging or "scolding". Acourt record from 1592 says …

The wife of Walter Hycocks and the wife of Peter Phillips are common scolds. Therefore it is ordered that they shall be told in church to stop their scolding. But, if their neighbours complain a second time, they shall be punished by the ducking stool.

And "the ducking stool" meant being tied to a chair and lowered into a nearby river.

10 If the ducking stool didn't work then there was the "branks" – an iron mask that clamped onto the head with a metal bar going into the woman's mouth to hold her tongue down. Wearing the branks, a woman would be paraded round the town to show other women what might happen to them.

Miss World - Tudor style

The Elizabethans had a clear idea of what a beautiful woman should look like. Here's a shopping list …

1 extremely white skin
2 blue eyes
3 ruby-red lips
4 fair hair

You don't fit the description? Never mind, you can always change if you want.

Dark hair can be bleached with a mixture of sulphur and lead. This will, unfortunately, make it fall out in time. Never mind, as an Elizabethan said, Elizabethan girls are …
not simply content with their own hair, but buy other hair either of horse, mare or any other strange beast,
Skin too dark? A deadly mixture of lead and vinegar can be plastered on. (This has the same effect as making an Egyptian mummy.)
Lips too pale? Lipstick could be made from egg whites and cochineal - what is "cochineal"? It's a dye made from crushed cochineal beetles.

THREE SIMPLE STEPS TO A MORE BEAUTIFUL YOU!

Eyes don't sparkle enough? Drop in some belladonna (which means, "beautiful lady"!) to make them look larger. Keep it away from your lips, though. Belladonna is a poisonous drug made from deadly-nightshade.

If a mother wanted her daughter to grow up beautiful she was advised to bathe her in milk to give her a pale skin. Unwanted freckles? (Definitely out of fashion.) Treat with "brimstone" (sulphur).

Smelly? **Don't** have a bath! (Baths aren't considered "healthy"!) Just cover up the smell with perfume.

So …

Would you like to have been a Tudor woman or girl? In fact, would you have liked to live in the Terrible Tudor times at all? The Golden Age" of Good Queen Bess and Jolly Old Henry VIII?

Every age has its problems. But, as a historian once said …
In reviewing the past I think that we of the present day have much to be thankful for.

You've reviewed some of the Tudor past in this book. So, are you "thankful" that you didn't live then? Or do you agree with the history book that said it was an extremely exciting time to be alive?

Epilogue

Old Elizabeth died and the last of the terrible Tudors was gone. Mary Queen of Scots was dead too … but her son, James VI of Scotland, was very much alive. The first of the sinister Stuarts.

The Stuart family in Scotland had a history every bit as bloody and violent as the Tudors in England.

• James I was murdered in a toilet in 1437 while he was trying to defend himself with a pair of fire tongs

• James II was killed by an exploding cannon in the seige of Roxburgh in 1460

• James III was murdered by his nobles in 1486

• James IV was killed at the Battle of Flodden in 1513

• James V died of despair shortly after his defeat at the battle of Solway Floss in 1542.

• Mary Queen of Scots, as we already know, murdered her husband then fled to England to avoid the chop. Elizabeth gave it to her instead

• James VI became the first James of England … and the first lucky Stuart to come from Scotland. He came south and added the English throne to his collection.

Of course, not everyone was happy with James. Not everyone wanted a king with such disgusting habits! For a start, he picked his nose!

James always wore a dagger-proof vest. Who can blame him? First, some cunning Catholics tried to blow him off the throne with the gunpowder plot. Lucky James survived again! We may forget James, but we always remember the fifth of November!

And that was just the start of a dramatic century. A century of plagues and fire and plots and rebels; a century with Englishmen fighting Englishmen and Englishmen hanging witches - the Scots preferred to burn them!

If the Tudors gave their queens a sharp pain in the neck then the Stuart people gave it to one of their kings!

The Stuart times were certainly sinister. But that's another story, and another slice of Horrible History...

TERRIBLE TUDORS

GRISLY QUIZ

Now find out if you're a
terrible Tudor expert!

HORRIBLE HENRY

Henry VIII was one of Britain's cruellest monarchs ever. Here's a quick quiz to test your brains. Get one wrong and your head goes on the block…

1. When wife no. 1, Catherine of Aragon, died Henry had a...?
a) ball
b) fight
c) cup of tea

2. Wife no. 2, Anne Boleyn, needed the toilet a lot during her coronation. Her ladies-in-waiting kept her potty handy...?
a) under the table
b) in a room close by
c) on the throne

3. When Anne gave birth to a daughter, Henry...?
a) sulked
b) cheered
c) fell out of his pram

4. While Anne was being beheaded, Henry was playing...?
a) tennis
b) music
c) the fool

5. Henry divorced wife no. 4, Anne of Cleves, because she was...?
a) ugly
b) stupid
c) vegetarian

6. Wife no. 5, Catherine Howard, was sentenced to death for having lovers. She begged for mercy but Heartless Henry locked the door and left her...?
a) to wail
b) in jail
c) looking pale

7. Henry had his old friend Thomas More executed and his head stuck...?
a) over London Bridge
b) under London Bridge
c) in a fridge

8. Henry had Cardinal Fisher beheaded and showed disrespect by leaving the headless body...?
a) naked for a day
b) on the main highway
c) in a window display

INGENIOUS INSULTS

Can you match the words in these columns to come up with ten insults that Shakespeare put into his plays? WARNING: Do NOT call your teacher any of these names.

1. taffeta	**a)** lump
2. scurvy	**b)** ape
3. red-tailed	**c)** chuff
4. threadbare	**d)** bumble-bee
5. mad-headed	**e)** punk
6. fat	**f)** juggler
7. false	**g)** crookback
8. bloodsucker of	**h)** caterpillars
9. scolding	**i)** sleeping men
10. deformed	**j)** lord

1. Catholic Mary came to the throne in 1553, and the Protestants showed what they thought of her by leaving something on her bed. What? (Clue: hounding her out of the palace?)

2. Mary married Spanish Prince Philip in 1554. He hated something that came from her nose. What? (Clue: 'snot what you think)

3. Philip left Mary and went to fight in Europe. She tried to tempt him back with what? (Clue: the way to a man's heart is through his stomach, they say)

4. Mary had a lot of Protestant 'heretics' burned. Her chief helper was Reginald Pole who chose really odd 'heretics' to burn. What was odd about them? (Clue: they never felt a thing)

5. Mary sent Archbishop Cranmer to the stake in 1556. He had written an apology then changed his mind. When he saw the fire he did a strange thing. What? (Clue: he went to his death single-handed)

6. Mary died and the news was taken to half-sister Elizabeth, the new queen. They say Elizabeth was reading in the garden when the news came, but that's unlikely. Why? (Clue: remember, remember when Mary died)

7. Elizabeth had a new tax created which only men could pay. It was a tax on what? (Clue: it might grow on you)

8. Elizabeth I's godson, Sir John Harrington, disgraced himself by making rude remarks to her ladies-in-waiting. She

banished him. He went off and invented something that was so useful she forgave him. What? (Clue: flushed with success?)

9. In 1576 the explorer Martin Frobisher returned to England with a load of 'black earth'. What use did he think it would be? (Clue: he thinks the soil is rich)

10. Eloye Mestrell invented the first machine in England for making coins for the government. Yet in 1578 he was arrested and executed. What was his crime? (Clue: double your money)

11. Mary Queen of Scots had Sir John Huntly beheaded but then discovered he had to be tried properly and found guilty if she was to get his fortune. What did she do? (Clue: head on over to the courtroom)

12. Mary Queen of Scots became unpopular in Scotland, and fled to England to ask cousin Elizabeth I for protection. How did Liz protect Mary? (Clue: no one can get in to get her)

13. James Douglas of Scotland invented the 'Maiden' machine. In 1581 the Maiden killed him. What was it? (Clue: a chip off the old block)

14. Mary Queen of Scots had lots of troubles. She finally met a man and thanked him for, 'making an end to all my troubles'. What was this man's job? (Clue: not an agony aunt!)

15. When Mary Queen of Scots was beheaded in 1587 her head was supposed to have been lifted high in the air by the executioner to prove she was dead. But he dropped it. Why? (Clue: hair today, gone tomorrow)

WOULD YOU BELIEVE IT?

Queen Elizabeth I ruled from 1558 to 1603. There are lots of stories about this famous queen, but which of these tall tales are true and which false...?
1. She threatened to pass a law banning her courtiers from wearing long cloaks.
2. She died because of a rotten tooth.
3. Elizabeth was overjoyed when her sister, Mary, died.
4. She liked to read her horoscope.
5. Elizabeth ate a chessboard.
6. She had regular baths.
7. Elizabeth never even considered getting married.
8. Elizabeth had beautiful red hair.
9. She was always true to her Protestant faith.
10. She punched and kicked her secretary.

Answers

Horrible Henry
1–8. All answers are (a). Anyone answering (c) should give up quizzes ... now.

Ingenious insults
1.e) 2.j) 3.d) 4.f) 5.b) 6.c) 7.h) 8.i) 9.g) 10.a)

Quick Questions – Mean Queens
1. A dead dog. The head was shaved, the ears cropped and a noose put around its neck. The message was clear: 'This is what we do to Catholics.'

2. Philip hated Mary's foul breath. It was an illness she had and not her fault. But it put him off, and he left her broken hearted.

3. His favourite meat pies. She had them sent across the English Channel to him. He ate all the pies but didn't go home for more.

4. They were dead. Reggie dug them up and burned them anyway. Funny feller.

5. He stuck his writing hand in the flames to punish it for writing the apology. (No jokes about second-hand shops, please.)

6. It was November. Not many people are daft enough to sit in the garden in an English winter.

7. Beards.

8. A flushing toilet. It took him six years to invent it but Liz loved his loo.

9. He believed it contained a fortune in gold. It didn't. He was just a clueless captain.

10. Eloye made a second, secret, machine and forged money for himself. Usually forgers had a hand chopped off but Eloye was hanged.

11. Huntly's head was sewn back on and his corpse was put on trial.

12. Elizabeth locked Mary in prison. She left her there for years before deciding to execute her.

13. The Maiden was a type of guillotine. He was executed on it.

14. He was her executioner. Actually he made a messy end to her troubles, taking three chops and a bit of sawing to get the head off

15. Mary was wearing a wig. When he grabbed it, the head slipped out and bounced on to the floor.

Would you believe it?
1. True. She was terrified of being killed and wanted her courtiers' swords uncovered and ready.
2. False. Elizabeth is famous for having rotten teeth, but that didn't kill her. She caught a cold and never recovered.
3. True. She said, 'This is the Lord's doing and it is marvellous in our eyes.'
4. True. A mathematician (and magician!) called John Dee used to read Liz's horoscope and foretell the future for her.
5. True. Of course, it was made of marzipan.
6. True. Elizabeth did bathe regularly ... once every three months!
7. False. Liz had a few close calls when it came to marriage, including Lord Dudley and the French Duke of Anjou.
8. True and False. She did at first, but she ended up bald with a collection of 80 wigs!
9. False. While Catholic Mary Tudor was queen, Elizabeth said she was a Catholic too.
10. True. Secretary William Davison was just one of the unfortunate palace workers who suffered Liz's temper tantrums.

INTERESTING INDEX

Where will you find 'blood-sucking fleas', 'smelly breath', 'swearing' and 'sewers' in an index? In a Horrible Histories book, of course!

Anne of Cleves (wife of Henry VIII) 11, 69
apothecaries (herbalists) 22
apprentices 44
aprons 116
armies, private 45

Babbington, Anthony (traitor) 75-6
babies
   dying 86
   unlucky 87
barbers (part-time surgeons) 22
bear baiting 95-6
beetles, for lipstick 122
beggars 35, 40, 49-50, 82, 84,
beheadings 11-14, 17, 19, 66, 74-5
bird pie 90-1
blood-letting (cure for illness) 22
Boleyn, Anne (wife of Henry VIII) 11-12, 14, 17, 66, 68
Bonaparte, Napoleon (emperor of France) 105
Bosworth Field, battle of 10, 16, 64
branks (head cages) 121
bribes 45
brimstone (sulphur) 123

Bull, Mrs (landlandy) 58-61, 63
burnings at stake 18

Catherine of Aragon (wife of Henry VIII) 11, 16, 66
Catholics 10, 12-13, 16, 18, 27, 37-9, 73-4, 107, 126
cats, drinking blood of 25
Cecil, William (lord) 70
changelings (wicked fairies) 86
Chattox, Anne (witch) 88
Church of England 10, 17, 27, 38
Clitheroe, John (butcher) 38
Clitheroe, Margaret (martyr) 38-40
Clusius (potato grower) 111
Cockatrice 94
cockfighting (at 10 Downing Street!) 66
codes, secret 76-7
Columbus, Christopher (Italian explorer) 16
conspirators 75
constables 46, 63
convents 119
corsets, iron 115
Cranmer, Thomas (archbishop of Canterbury) 18

crimes 35-51
curses 54, 83-4

Davison, William (Elizabeth I's secretary) 72, 74
death
  by crushing 39-40
  sentences 36
  warrants 74
divorce 10-11, 69
doctors 22-4
Drake, Francis 19, 104-7, 113
Drake's Drum 105-6
drugs, poisonous 123
ducking stools 121

Edward VI (king) 9, 12, 14, 17-18, 79
Egyptian mummies 122
Elizabeth I (queen) 9, 13, 15, 17-19, 33-4, 38, 43, 68, 70-9, 104-7, 111, 116, 124-5
Elizabeth of York (queen) 10
entrails 19
Essex, Earl of (rebel leader) 13, 19, 72, 77
executions see beheadings

fairies, wicked 86
Field of the Cloth of Gold (famous meeting between Henry VIII and Francis I of France) 67
fireboats 108
Fitzherbert, Anthony (writer) 120
fleas, blood-sucking 25
football (Tudor-style)
France 73-4, 111, 114
Francis, Elizabeth (witch) 80-1
Francis I (king of France) 17, 67
Frizer, Ingram (trickster) 58, 61-2
fustigation (beating) 24

games 28, 95-103
Gerard, John (writer) 111
ghosts 88
gold, plundered 104
greed 93-4
Grey, Jane (nine-day queen) 12, 18
guilds (craftsmen's groups) 33, 44
gunpowder plot 126

hair 44, 71, 122
hamsters 52
hangings 16, 19, 29, 38, 61, 81, 84-5, 88, 114, 126
hares 87, 89
Harkett, Margaret (witch) 82-5
Harrison, William (writer) 112
heads
  in cages 121
  cut off (see beheadings)
  on poles 36
Henry VII (king) 9-10, 12, 14, 16, 64-5, 73, 79
Henry VIII (king) 8-11, 14, 16-17, 27, 34, 43, 65-8, 79, 89, 93, 103, 115, 119, 124
Hitler, Adolf (German leader) 106
Hoffman, Calvin (professor) 56
hose (trousers) 115, 117
Howard, Catherine (wife of Henry VIII) 11, 14
Howard, Lord (admiral) 109

insults 52-3
James VI/I (king of Scotland/England) 112, 125-6
Justices of the Peace (law enforcers) 40-5

Kett, Robert (revolting landowner) 17, 19
kidnappings 36
Kings of Scotland 125
Kyd, Thomas ("friend" of Marlowe) 61-2

Lancaster Family 65
laws
 against football/golf 103
 against clothes 116
 dodging 45
 enforcing 40-5
 witchcraft 86
leeches (blood-suckers) 22
Lisle, Humphrey (thief) 36-7
Louis XIV (king of France) 78

magic 46, 86, 105
Marlowe, Christopher (playwright) 57-63
marriage 77-8, 80, 119
Mary I (queen) 9, 12-13, 15, 18, 79, 106
Mary (queen of Scots) 12-13, 18-19, 73-7, 107, 125
Mary Rose (Henry VIII's warship) 89
mastiffs, mauled 95-6
meat, rotten 89
monasteries 10, 17, 27

Northumberland, Duke of (protector) 12, 17

parliament 65, 116
Parr, Catherine (wife of Henry VIII) 11
peacocks, skinned 94
pen-knives 31-2
Philip II (king of Spain) 13, 18, 75, 106-7
plague 25
Platter, Thomas (writer) 120
Poley (spy) 58-9, 61-2
Popes 10, 38
postal service 33
potatoes 111
priests 39, 52
printing press 37
Protestants 12-13, 15-16, 18, 38, 73, 109

punishments 28-9, 35-51
 for beliefs 61
 for crimes 41-3
 for long hair 44
 for witchcraft 86
 for women 120-1
puritans 115

quill pens, making 31-2

Raleigh, Walter (sailor) 110-12
recipes, revolting 90-2
recusants (those not attending church) 38
Reformation 38
relics 37
religion 37-40
Rich, Barnaby (writer) 112
Richard III (king) 7, 10, 14, 16, 64-5
riots 40
Roses, Wars of 16, 65
Royal Navy 105
ruffs
 making 118
 stiff 114-15
 wearing 117

sailors, legendary 104-13
Satan 80
schools 26-34, 119
scolds (nags) 121
Scotland/Scottish 36, 45, 73, 75, 103, 126
scurvy 89
sewers 20
Seymour, Jane (wife of Henry VIII) 11, 66, 68
Shakespeare, William (playwright) 18, 52-7, 63-4, 117
sheep 19, 80
Simnel, Lambert (pretender to throne) 16

Skeres (robber) 58-9, 61-2
skulls
    digging up 88
    of executed criminals 25
    swallowing powdered 24
slavery 36
slippers, throwing 72
smelly breath 89
Somerset, Duke of (protector) 12, 17
Spain 73-5, 106-9
Spanish Armada 19, 75, 104, 106-9
spiders, buttered 24
spies 33, 76
spoons, extra-long 114
sports
    blood 95-6
    school 31
Stanley (lord) 64
Star Chamber (Court of law) 45
Stuarts 19, 90, 125-6
Stubbes, Philip (puritan) 115
swearing 30

table manners 93
Tate, Nahum (writer) 53
taxes 43, 116
teeth
    bears' 95
    picking 93
    rotten 71
tobacco 111-12
toilets
    hole in ground 20
    murder in 125
torture 39, 52, 62, 88, 95-6

Walsingham, Francis (spy/secretary) 72, 76
Walsingham, Thomas (friend of Marlowe) 61

Warbeck, Perkin (pretender to throne) 16
Waterhouse, Agnes (witch) 81
Waterloo, battle of 105
witch-finder general 88
witches 68, 80-8, 126
wizards 46
wool trade 43, 116
World Wars 105-6
Wyatt, Thomas (rebel leader) 13

York Family 65

Terry Deary was born at a very early age, so long ago he can't remember. But his mother, who was there at the time, says he was born in Sunderland, north-east England, in 1946 – so it's not true that he writes all *Horrible Histories* from memory. At school he was a horrible child only interested in playing football and giving teachers a hard time. His history lessons were so boring and so badly taught, that he learned to loathe the subject. *Horrible Histories* is his revenge.

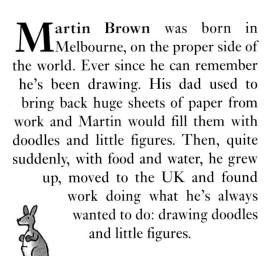

Martin Brown was born in Melbourne, on the proper side of the world. Ever since he can remember he's been drawing. His dad used to bring back huge sheets of paper from work and Martin would fill them with doodles and little figures. Then, quite suddenly, with food and water, he grew up, moved to the UK and found work doing what he's always wanted to do: drawing doodles and little figures.

Make sure you've got the whole horrible lot!

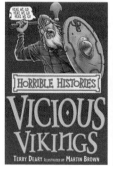

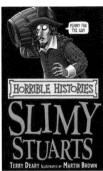

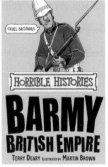

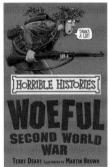

To run the Terrible Tudors CD-ROM on your computer:

PC
Insert the disc into your CD-ROM drive
Terrible Tudors should start automatically
If you do not have autorun switched on, select Start > Run
Type D:\Tudors.exe where D is the letter of your CD-ROM drive

MAC
Insert the disc into your CD-ROM drive
Open the Terrible Tudors CD-ROM on your desktop
Double click the icon labelled Terrible Tudors

Note: You will require Adobe Reader in order to be able to access and print some of the downloadable features on this disc. If you do not have Adobe Reader, you can download it for free at: http://www.adobe.com/products/acrobat/readstep2.html

If you have any difficulties, please refer to common help issues at our support site: http://www.fifthdimension.com/support/hh-terribletudors

MINIMUM SYSTEM REQUIREMENTS
The following are the minimum system requirements to run the Terrible Tudors CD-ROM

PC
Pentium® III 800 MHz processor
Microsoft® Windows® 2000, XP, Vista
512 MB RAM available

MAC
Mac running OS 10.4 or higher, with 256Mb Ram
• iMac
• iBook
• Power Macintosh
• G3 PowerBook
• Power Mac G4 Cube
• Any other PowerBook introduced after May 1998

PLUS
32 bit colour monitor capable of displaying 1024 x 768 resolution
12x CD-ROM Drive
Sound card
Headphones or speakers
Mouse or compatible optical pointing device
Printer
Adobe Reader